MW01137501

NATIONAL PARK

By Tom Carter

DAYHIKING PRESS
GARLAND, TEXAS

ABOUT THE AUTHOR

The day after his high school graduation in 1973, Tom Carter left Arkansas and headed for Wyoming. What began as a summer job grew into a lifetime love affair with the great outdoors.

For six summers Tom guided tours through the Yellowstone-Grand Teton area. During that time, he developed a passion for hiking. Two thousand miles and three pair of hiking boots later, Tom wrote *DAY HIKING YELLOWSTONE* to help fellow employees get into and enjoy the backcountry. For years it was given free of charge to all interested employees and in 1985 it became available to the general public. *DAY HIKING GRAND TETON NATIONAL PARK*, Tom's second interpretive guide, was first published in 1993 and *DAY HIKING THE WIND RIVER RANGE*, followed in 1997. These popular guides have given over 100,000 day hikers an educational and enjoyable way to experience the Greater Yellowstone Ecosystem.

Following in the footsteps of Teddy "The Trust Buster" Roosevelt, Tom is an attorney in the Southwest Region of the Federal Trade Commission in Dallas, Texas, where he participates in the antitrust and consumer protection activities of the FTC in five states. But no matter where life leads him, Tom's heart will never be far from these backcountry trails.

ACKNOWLEDGMENTS

I want to especially thank Sharlene Milligan, former Executive Director for the Grand Teton Natural History Association and Dick DuMais, owner of High Peak Books for their expert advice and assistance. Thanks to my good friend Jeff Crabtree, owner of Skinny Skis in Jackson, and Lana, Katie, and Shane Crabtree for their friendship and support over the years. I also want to acknowledge Shelli & Jerry Johnson, publishers of the Yellowstone Journal and Lee Whittlesey, Yellowstone Park Historian. As always, I'm indebted to my friend Bruce Lott for his typesetting and computer support.

Thanks to my dad, Clayton, my wife, Judy, and my daughter, Cortney, for their support and encouragement. Finally, to all my Yellowstone friends who put up with me over the years, thanks for the memories.

CONTENTS

INTRODUCTION

The Tetons truly have something for everyone! People are naturally drawn to them. For hundreds of years Indian tribes, including the Crow, Nez Perce, Shoshone and Gros Ventre frequented the Teton region. During the early 1800's, most of the great mountain men, including John Colter, Jim Bridger, David Jackson and Jedediah Smith, passed beneath these mountains. Later came Thomas Moran, Teddy Roosevelt, John D. Rockefeller and Ansel Adams. These and many millions of others have been touched by the Teton's rugged peaks, awesome canyons, sparkling clear alpine lakes, plentiful wildlife, powerful glaciers and spectacular wildflower displays.

This trail guide contains mile by mile descriptions, including history, geology, plant and wildlife facts and brief anecdotes, for 15 of the best hikes in the park. These cover almost 50 miles of trails carefully chosen to give you the best wilderness experience for the effort. Before you head out, carefully review:

1) The Trail Selector Chart—to find which hikes contain the most features which interest you;

2) The Trail Summaries section—to learn the time, distance, elevation gain and degree of difficulty involved;

3) The Trailhead Locator Map—to get a general idea of where each hike begins; and

4) The brief discussions provided concerning park rules, dangers to expect and equipment needs.

The best way to experience the Tetons is on foot. It's more than just a means of travel. It's a process of growth—a way of learning more about yourself. Attitude, awareness, freedom and satisfaction matter more than how far, how fast or how high you climb. Hiking can bring you closer to the wilderness, closer to God and closer to yourself. So take time and enjoy!

🐾 TOM CARTER

TRAIL SELECTOR CHART

This will help you select hikes containing features which interest you:

HIKE #	1	2	3	4	5	6	7	8	9	10	11	12	13	14	15
In Mountains				●	●				●	●	●	●	●	●	●
In Valley	●	●	●			●	●	●							
View of Grand			●		●		●		●	●			●	●	
River or Stream			●		●				●	●		●	●	●	●
Lake	●	●			●	●	●	●	●	●	●		●		●
Canyon					●				●	●		●	●		●
Water Fall					●				●	●		●	●		
Wildlife			●								●			●	
Wild-flowers				●									●		●
Unique Geology					●				●						
Interesting History		●	●											●	
Overnight Camping						●		●	●		●	●	●	●	●
Off Trail Hiking			●							●		●			
Boat or Tram Fee				●	●					●			●		●

TRAIL SUMMARIES

HIKES	ROUNDTRIP MILES	ELEVATION GAIN*	HIKING TIME	DIFFICULTY
SHORT HIKES & EASY WALKS				
① Colter Bay Nature Trail	1.8 mi.	50 ft.	1.5 hr.	Easy
② Lunchtree Hill/Willow Flats	1 mi.	100 ft.	1 hr.	Easy
③ Schwabacher's Landing	1 mi.	20 ft.	1 hr.	Easy
④ Rendezvous Mountain	1.2 mi.	530 ft.	1 hr.**	Moderate
⑤ Hidden Falls/Inspiration Pt.	2 mi.	420 ft.	1.5 hr.**	Moderate
HALF-DAY HIKES				
⑥ String & Leigh Lakes	5 mi.	40 ft.	2.5 hr.	Easy
⑦ Taggart & Bradley Lakes	5 mi.	530 ft.	3 hr.	Moderate
⑧ Hermitage Point	9.5 mi.	130 ft.	5 hr.	Moderate
⑨ Death Canyon	8 mi.	1,050 ft.	5 hr.	Strenuous
⑩ Hanging Canyon	6 mi.	2,800 ft.	5 hr.**	Very Strenuous
FULL-DAY HIKES				
⑪ Amphitheater Lake	11 mi.	3,100 ft.	7 hr.	Very Strenuous
⑫ Garnet Canyon	10 mi.	2,650 ft.	6 hr.	Strenuous
⑬ Lake Solitude	14.8 mi.	2,300 ft.	8 hr.**	Strenuous
⑭ Table Mountain	12 mi.	4,100 ft.	8 hr.	Very Strenuous
⑮ Marion Lake/Granite Canyon	15.5 mi.	-4,150 ft.	8 hr.**	Strenuous

* The elevation difference between the hike's high point and low point. For a complete elevation profile see the elevation chart provided with the text of each hike.

TRAILHEAD LOCATOR MAP

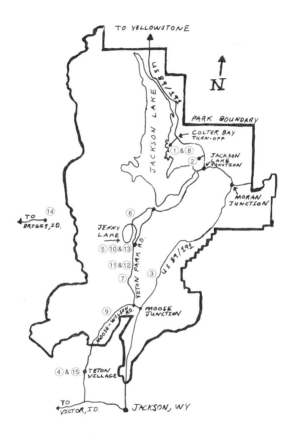

GRAND TETON NATIONAL PARK

FOLLOW THE RULES

Backcountry regulations have been established by the National Park Service to preserve the natural beauty of the Tetons and to protect the hikers who wish to experience it. ***Knowing these regulations is extremely important.*** Following them can make your backcountry adventure safe and enjoyable.

Always check-in at a NPS Ranger Station before beginning your hike. The Rangers are there to help you. They can tell you about trail conditions and any special hazards or restrictions. If you plan to camp overnight, you must get a Backcountry Use Permit at the Moose or Colter Bay Visitor Centers or the Jenny Lake Ranger Station.

Some Teton "Do's and Don'ts":

DO discuss your itinerary with a Ranger before leaving.

DO purchase a Wyoming fishing license before trying your luck.

DO acquire a free Backcountry Use Permit for overnight trips and camp only in designated camping zones.

DO suspend your surplus food in a tree overnight and take other bear precautions.

DON'T build campfires except at designated lakeshore campsites.

DON'T bring firearms, pets, mountain bikes, or motorized vehicles into the backcountry.

DON'T litter trails or pollute streams (even soap pollutes).

DON'T disturb or feed wildlife.

DON'T pick wildflowers or collect souvenirs.

DON'T shortcut switchbacks on the trail.

LEAVE YOUR CAMP CLEAN. TAKE NOTHING BUT PICTURES. LEAVE NOTHING BUT FOOTPRINTS

BEWARE OF DANGERS

The Teton trails contain many hazards not commonly encountered. You need not be afraid of the backcountry, but you better respect it. Remember, a little common sense goes a long way. Be prepared and be careful. **The following discussion will assist you in preparing for backcountry hazards:**

WEATHER

Lightning storms occur frequently. Quickly get off exposed ridges. Avoid streams, puddles, isolated trees or rocks, and open meadows. If caught in the open, crouch low, head down, with only your feet touching the ground.

Exposure to wind, rain and/or cold temperatures can result in **hypothermia**. This rapid loss of body heat can cause severe damage and even kill, if not properly treated. Wear warm clothing, stay dry and protect yourself from strong winds. Early symptoms include: shivering, slurred speech, memory lapses, stumbling, drowsiness and exhaustion. **Treat even mild symptoms immediately and aggressively.** Get out of the wind and rain. Replace wet clothes with dry ones, drink warm sweetened liquids, get in a warm sleeping bag, stay awake. Once you are warmed up and able to travel, return quickly to civilization.

Sunburn is a common injury in the mountains. At this elevation, the sun is more powerful. If you are turning pink, you are already burned. Cover all the burned areas immediately. **Use high rated sunscreen on exposed skin, and a moisturizer on your lips.** Sunglasses are also essential.

Heat exhaustion can be disabling. When hiking in dry hot areas, wear light clothing and drink one to two quarts of water per day.

DRINKING WATER

Lakes and streams in the Tetons may contain bacteria, viruses and microscopic organisms called *Giardia lamblia*, which cause severe intestinal disorders and diarrhea. To be safe, it is best to carry sufficient

domestically treated water from park drinking fountains or water spigots
Take at least one quart per person per half day. If you must use wate
from lakes or streams, boil for at least one minute to kill harmfu
organisms or pass it through a filter system labeled Giardia-effective wit
a mesh no larger than one micron.

ALTITUDE SICKNESS

At higher elevations, the air pressure is low, causing your body to g
1/4 to 1/3 less oxygen than at sea level. Watch for signs of altitud
sickness such as headaches, impaired memory and extreme shortness c
breath. The body can partially compensate for the "thinner" air, b
acclimation takes weeks. Those used to lower elevations should tak
special care not to overexert. **Start out slowly and work up to that b**
hike.

ROCK CLIMBING

In the Tetons, leaving established trails can be dangerous. U
extreme caution when near cliffs and when traversing boulder fields ar
open talus slopes. **Never attempt technical rock climbing witho**
proper training and equipment. Turn back if trail, rock or sno
conditions make your trip less than reasonably safe. A mountain searc
and rescue team is available during summer months to assist those wl
are seriously injured or stranded. In the mountains an SOS call is
signals of any kind repeated at regular intervals. This can be audible
visible—three shouts, three flashes from a light, etc.

SNOW CONDITIONS

The upper reaches of the Teton Range receive many feet of snow ea
winter. Sections of the higher elevation trails described in this gui
may be covered with snow and ice until mid-summer. Conditions va
form year to year, so check with a ranger before leaving. **Use cauti**
when snow is encountered and never walk out on snow slopes whi
lie above rocks or cliffs. Turn back if the trail is blocked by a sno
cornice or conditions appear less than safe.

LOST

If you become lost, **stay calm**. Sit down, think through the situatic
Check your map and compass. The solution may become obvious.

Plan first, then act. Perhaps some backtracking will put you on the trail. When all else fails, follow creeks downstream. They eventually lead to drainages, which will cross other trails, or lead to civilization.

ANIMALS

The Tetons provide habitat for black bear and on rare occasions, grizzly. Bears are particularly dangerous when startled, when cubs are present or when approached too closely. To avoid injury, **do not hike alone or after daylight hours.** Make noise as you hike to reduce the chance of surprising a bear. On overnight trips, seal surplus food in a plastic bag and suspend between two trees at least ten (10) feet above the ground, sleep away from your kitchen and don't sleep in your cooking clothes. Avoid all scented cosmetics, perfumes and deodorants, which may attract bears.

If you spot a bear, slowly back away and make a wide detour around it. **If confronted by a bear, stay calm. Do not run.** Running may cause a bear to chase you. If a bear charges, stand your ground. Usually the bear will stop before making contact. After the bear stops, you should back away slowly. If the bear continues, your last resort may be to play dead. Climbing trees provides little or no protection from black bears, since they are excellent climbers.

Avoid other large animals such as moose, elk, buffalo, and wolves. These animals are extremely dangerous at close range, especially during mating season or when young animals are present. Even small animals, such as chipmunks and squirrels can be a threat if they carry rabies or other contagious diseases. And until mid-August there's always a risk of being carried off by killer mosquitoes. So be prepared!

BACKCOUNTRY EQUIPMENT

BOOTS . . . a good pair, is the most important piece of equipment you can own. They should protect your feet from rocks and moisture, support your ankles and arches, and provide good traction on a variety of surfaces. In the Tetons, you can use anything from a high-tech, lightweight (2 lbs.) "psychedelic running shoe" to a heavy-duty climbing boot (4-5 lbs.).

A BACKPACK . . . will be your home in the backcountry. A daypack is all you will need for the hikes described in this guide. However, for longer hikes and overnight trips, you may want a frame pack.

CLOTHING . . . will protect you from the elements while you are on the trail. Teton weather can change dramatically. Be prepared! Take along raingear and several layers of clothes that can be added or shed as the weather requires. A good combination would include a T-shirt, a long sleeved shirt, a down vest or wind-breaker, and a rain parka. A hat is also handy to keep the high altitude sun off your head and out of your eyes.

TRAILS ILLUSTRATED MAPS & GPS

TOPOGRAPHIC MAPS . . . are essential equipment. This guide book is coordinated for use with the **Trails Illustrated topo map of Grand Teton National Park**. Hike numbers appear on the Trails Illustrated map denoting the trailhead for each of the 15 hikes described in this guide. Both the map and this guide use an identical numbering system for hikes for cross referencing. Certain off-trail routes described in this guide are shown (in brown) on the Trails Illustrated map.

For each of the 15 hikes, this guide includes part of a 7.5-minute USGS topo map (for short hikes) or part of the full Park topo (for longer hikes). However it is recommended that you purchase the Trails Illustrated map. It will give you a much broader picture of the area you are exploring.

GLOBAL POSITIONING SYSTEM (GPS) . . . satellites encircle the earth and transmit precise position information. With a hand-held GPS receiver to triangulate the satellites, it is possible to pinpoint, within a few feet, your exact Latitude and Longitude anywhere in the world. These popular navigation devices literally put the whole world in your hands. This guide provides GPS locations for each hike's trailhead (in degrees, minutes and seconds north of the Equator and west of the Prime Meridian). This will assist users in confirming they are at the proper trailhead and could help lost hikers find their way home.

① COLTER BAY NATURE TRAIL

Early morning serenity of Jackson Lake.

TRAILHEAD: The trail begins at the north end of the Colter Bay Visitor Center, situated on the east side of Jackson Lake. From Jackson Lake Junction, take U.S. Highway 89/191 north 5.5 miles, turn left onto the Colter Bay Village Road and follow the signs to the Visitor Center. (GPS: 43° 54' 10" N, 110° 38' 38" W)

DISTANCE: 1.8 miles (round-trip).

ELEVATION CHANGES: 50 feet.

TIME REQUIRED: 1.5 hours.

DIFFICULTY: Easy.

COMMENTS: This pleasant loop hike takes you along the north side of Colter Bay, through lodgepole pine forests and out to the shore of Jackson Lake. It incorporates a 15 stop self-guided nature trail established by the National Park Service.

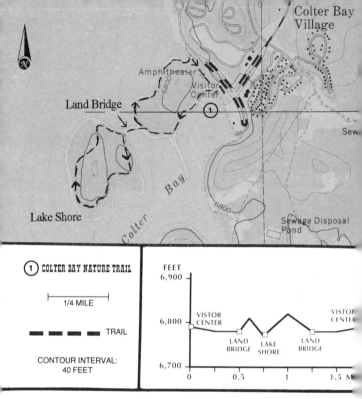

The trail begins at the north end of the Colter Bay Visitor Center, where an asphalt path leads down to the shore of Colter Bay. From there, you can easily follow the signs to the Colter Bay "Self-Guided Nature Trail."

The forest in this area is composed principally of lodgepole pine. This tall, straight, slender tree was commonly used by Indians in constructing their lodges, hence the name "lodgepole." Because the tree's root system contains no large center tap root, the strong winds which whip across Jackson Lake have toppled many mature trees. There, also, are a number of dead or dying lodgepole pines still standing. These are victims of the mountain pine bark beetle, which feeds on the living cambium layer of the tree just beneath the bark. Such occurrences are nature's way of maintaining the delicate balance of her ecosystem. These trees will slowly rot and decay, returning vital nutrients to the soil. In the meantime, they provide a home for many insects and small animals which in turn attract larger animals that feed on them. Thus, all things, no matter how large or small, are harmoniously combined in nature's grand scheme.

About a half mile from the Visitor Center, the trail turns left and crosses a narrow land-bridge out to what is essentially an island in Jackson Lake. The nature trail circles clockwise around the island, passing some 15 points of interest. An inexpensive brochure that describes these points can be picked up from a box located near the first point of interest.

Colter Bay was named in honor of John Colter, believed to be the first white man to lay eyes on the Tetons. He journeyed west as a member of the 1804 -1806 Lewis and Clark expedition, then decided to stay. Although just a private on the expedition, Colter impressed Lewis and Clark, who granted Colter's request for a discharge because "we were disposed to be of service to anyone of our party who had performed their duty as well as Colter." After assisting in the establishment of a trading post at the confluence of the Yellowstone and Bighorn rivers, Colter set out, in the winter of 1807-1808, to spread the word to the Crow Indian Nation that they could trade their pelts for blankets, beads and tobacco. It was on this remarkable trek that Colter is believed to have visited what is today Grand Teton and Yellowstone national parks.

About .9 miles from the Visitor Center the trail breaks out of the trees and affords nice views of the Tetons and Jackson Lake. This is the largest lake in the park, covering some 25,000 acres with a maximum depth of 445 feet. Over the years, this beautiful lake has borne many names. An 1814 map by Captain William Clark referred to it as "Lake Bittle" after Nicholas Bittle, editor of Lewis and Clark's journals. Trapper Joe Meek called it "Lewis Lake." It was known to some as "Teton Lake." However, the name that would stick was bestowed upon it in 1829 by fur trapper William Sublette, honoring his friend and partner David E. Jackson. Jackson Lake lies in a depression scooped out by glaciers and partially dammed by humans. The dam, originally constructed by the U.S. Bureau of Reclamation in 1916, raised the lake 39 feet above its natural level. As part of an arrangement worked out prior to the establishment of the National Park, the water rights to Jackson Lake belong to Idaho farmers. The lack of vegetation along the shore line is a result of fluctuating water levels caused by the annual release of water for irrigation purposes.

As the trail continues you are afforded sweeping views of the Teton Range. The two southern-most visible peaks are Teewinot (12,325'), a Shoshone Indian word meaning "many pinnacles," and the Grand Teton (13,770'). The next prominent mountain to the north is the flat-topped Mount Moran (12,605') named for Thomas Moran, the famous landscape artist who's many sketches and watercolors brought much notoriety to the Yellowstone-Grand Teton area in the 1870's. Further north are Bivouac (10,825'), Eagles Rest (11,258') and Ranger (11,355') peaks. Directly across the lake, between Eagles Rest and Ranger Peak, is Waterfalls Canyon. If you look carefully, you can see impressive Wilderness Falls, about two-thirds the way up the canyon with beautiful Columbine Cascades just below.

As you continue, look for stands of white-barked, quaking aspen trees. Listen . . . can you hear them "quake"? A very slight breeze causes the leaves to rustle, creating shimmering sounds similar to a small brook. This special quality is primarily due to the flat, rather than tubular, construction of the petiole (stem) which connects the broad flat leaf to the branch of the tree. The flat edge catches the wind and is much more flexible than the common tubular shape, thus allowing the leaves to rustle much more easily.

Just before the trail completes the loop of the island, look for a light green shrub about 8-10 inches high with tiny egg-shaped leaves and minute red berries. These grouse whortleberries, which ripen in early August, are extremely flavorful for their size. They are terrific in muffins and pancakes or simply for munching along the trail.

To conclude this loop hike, cross back over the land-bridge, turn left and return to the trailhead via a .5 mile route which takes you first along the lake shore, then branches off to the right through the trees. Look for signs directing you to the "Amphitheater" and "Visitor Center."

② LUNCHTREE HILL/WILLOW FLATS

Overlooking a quiet pond on the edge of Willow Flats.

TRAILHEAD: The trail begins at Jackson Lake Lodge located 1 mile north of Jackson Lake Junction on U.S. Highway 89/191. As you exit the rear of the lodge, take a right and follow the asphalt path up Lunchtree Hill. (GPS: 43° 52' 41" N, 110° 34' 40" W)

DISTANCE: 1 mile (round-trip).

ELEVATION CHANGES: 100 feet.

TIME REQUIRED: 1 hour.

DIFFICULTY: Easy.

COMMENTS: This short hike takes you to the top of Lunchtree Hill, then continues along an unofficial, unmarked, but well-traveled path which skirts the edge of the bluff above Willow Flats. This is the best hike in the park from which to observe moose. Jackson Lake Lodge, with its grand picture window overlooking Mount Moran (12,605'), is itself an impressive attraction. John D. Rockefeller, Jr. personally supervised its construction in 1955. To be certain the mountains were framed just right, he had a temporary scaffolding of the window erected prior to the building's construction.

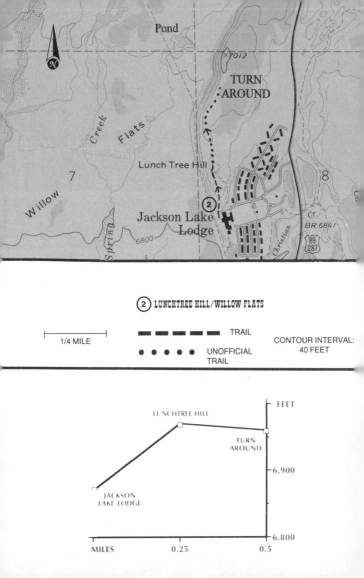

Pond

×7012

TURN
AROUND

Creek   Flats

Lunch Tree Hill

Willow

Spring

Christian

Cr

BR 684

② Jackson Lake
Lodge

6800

6800

7

8

89
287

② LUNCHTREE HILL/WILLOW FLATS

| 1/4 MILE | ▬ ▬ ▬ ▬ ▬ TRAIL | CONTOUR INTERVAL: |
| | ● ● ● ● ● UNOFFICIAL TRAIL | 40 FEET |

FEET

LUNCHTREE HILL

TURN
AROUND

6,900

JACKSON
LAKE LODGE

6,800

MILES   0.25   0.5

To begin the hike, pass through the lobby of Jackson Lake Lodge and exit on to the rear grounds, turn right and follow the path marked "Lunchtree Hill Loop Trail." As you climb the hill, scan the flat, bottom-land which stretches out toward Jackson Lake. These willow thickets and marshy meadows are excellent moose habitat. Although the moose is the largest member of the deer family and commonly attains a weight of 900 pounds, here in Willow Flats their large dark bodies seem to appear and disappear among the willows with graceful suddenness. The name "moose" comes from an Algonquin Indian term meaning "twig eater." These curious-looking creatures are highly specialized for this aquatic habitat. Their long legs allow them to move more freely about the marsh and feed on the leaves, bark and twigs of their most important food source, the willow. Their body even secretes an oil which makes their coat more water repellent.

You may also spot a sandhill crane in among the willows. These light-brown birds stand as tall as a mule deer and have a maximum wingspan of 6 feet. Long-legged and long-necked, they look similar to the great blue heron, but can be distinguished by a red patch on the head. Listen for their shrill musical rachet-like call.

Soon you will reach the top of Lunchtree Hill. It was on this site in 1926 that John D. Rockefeller, Jr., his family and Horace Albright, then superintendent of Yellowstone, shared a historic picnic lunch. Rockefeller was deeply moved by what he described as "quite the grandest and most spectacular mountains I have ever seen . . . a picture of ever-changing beauty which is to me beyond compare." Albright shared with Rockefeller his vision of expanding the national park system to include the Tetons. That vision was eventually realized, but not until after almost 25 years of controversy and compromise. The initial park, which was created by Congress in 1929, provided protection only for the area immediately surrounding the highest peaks. In the end, it was Rockefeller's generous gift of over 32,000 acres, acquired over many years, that enabled the park to be expanded to include the valley of Jackson Hole.

Rockefeller, who was also instrumental in the creation of Acadia, Redwood, Great Smoky Mountain, and Shenandoah national parks was honored in 1972 by the creation of the John D. Rockefeller, Jr. Memorial Parkway which lies between Yellowstone and Grand Teton national parks. In 1991, Albright was recognized for his important role in creating Grand Teton National Park when a 10,552 foot peak at the mouth of Death Canyon was named in his honor.

From the top of Lunchtree Hill, continue straight along the edge of the bluff which overlooks Willow Flats. Although there is no officially maintained trail, you should have no problem following the well-worn social use path which begins here. Notice the stark contrast between the vegetation along the path and that beneath you in the flats. These two areas are good examples of two distinct biotic communities in Jackson Hole—the sagebrush community and the willow community. The sagebrush community is actually one of the more complex of the dozen or so communities found in the park. It contains over 100 plant and animal species, including many colorful wildflowers such as the yellow arrowleaf balsamroot, several varieties of violet-colored asters, bright red Indian paintbrush and scarlet gilia, blue harebell, and purple lupine. Animals that frequent the sagebrush community include antelope, Uinta ground squirrel and snowshoe hare. The much wetter willow community occurs in areas where the water table is very near the soil surface. Willows, forbs, sedges and other aquatic plants predominate. In addition to the moose, the willow community attracts populations of beaver, muskrat and otter.

Jackson Hole and the rugged Teton peaks which lie beyond have inspired many a photographer, including noted landscape artist Ansel Adams. So compelling are Adams' images of the Tetons that one was included in the payload of the Voyager II spacecraft in an effort to convey the beauty of our planet to lifeforms beyond our solar system. Now that's a picture that is "out of this world."

You should turn around at the half-mile point, where the trail drops a bit and dissipates as it enters the trees. The white-barked aspen trees found in this area often form another distinct biotic community. As you see here, aspen trees commonly grow closely together in stands. New trees sprout from the roots of older trees, particularly following a forest fire. Aspens rarely grow older than 200 years of age and actually begin to deteriorate after just 80 years. Due to suppression of forest fires, the aspens in the park are aging and becoming increasingly infested with disease and insects. This in turn attracts myriad of birds including woodpeckers, robins, mountain bluebirds, swallows, nuthatches and chickadees. Before you return, take a moment to count how many different birds you can hear or see among the aspens.

Nature's engineers at work.

TRAILHEAD: This short walk begins at a raft launch site on the Snake River, located 4 miles north of Moose Junction and 14 miles south of Moran Junction on U.S. Highway 89/191. Turn west on a small dirt road marked "Schwabacher Landing Road" and proceed one mile to the end. An unmarked, but well-beaten path leads upstream from the parking area along a small side channel of the Snake River. (GPS: 43° 42' 46" N, 110° 40' 15" W)

DISTANCE: 1 mile (round-trip).

ELEVATION CHANGES: 20 Feet.

TIME REQUIRED: 1 hour.

DIFFICULTY: Easy.

COMMENTS: This easy walk follows an unofficial, unmaintained, social use path which travels along one of the many small side channels of the Snake River. It gives you a glimpse of the wild beauty of one of the most prominent waterways in the great northwest and affords an excellent opportunity to observe the industrious beaver and his engineering handiwork. **Note: beaver are not always active in this area. Dams often wash away and are replaced elsewhere.** 21

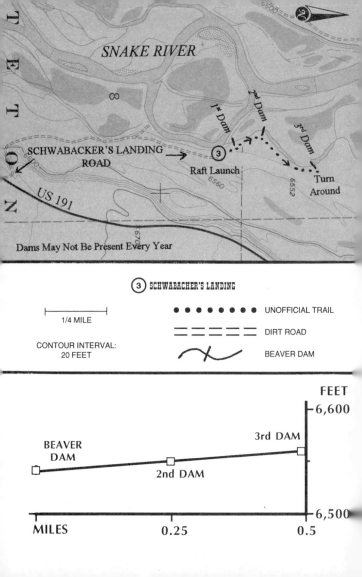

You will immediately observe the first of three beaver dams and a beaver lodge. As you can see, beaver have a dramatic impact on their surroundings. Their dams reduce the flow of water, drown trees and create an environment conducive to many aquatic plants, like the beautiful yellow monkeyflowers which occasionally are found lining the banks of the channel. In addition, water fowl, including Canada geese, mallards and goldeneye ducks, and mammals such as muskrat, otter and moose thrive in this beaver engineered environment.

The beaver's powerful jaws and sharp teeth enable it to cut a five-inch tree in under five minutes and occasionally fall trees up to two feet in diameter. To construct a dam, they poke felled logs into the streambed, then pile sticks, mud and gravel around them. The resulting pond covers the subterranean entrance to their lodge, making it almost impregnable. The lodge itself starts out as a solid mound of sticks and mud, then rooms and various escape tunnels are gnawed out from the inside.

A second, older, and much less prominent beaver dam, is encountered about 1/4 mile from the trailhead. As you continue along the path which parallels the channel watch closely for beaver. Although they are nocturnal, they can sometimes be spotted during the day. The best time to observe them is in the morning or late in the evening, around twilight. Beaver, which weigh up to sixty pounds, are the largest rodents in North America and are extremely well-suited for their aquatic life. They are excellent swimmers using their broad flat tail and partially webbed hind feet for propulsion. They can stay underwater for up to fifteen minutes and are equipped with special transparent membranes which cover their eyes, allowing them to see well under water. They even have an oil gland which allows them to waterproof their heavy fur coat.

Unfortunately for the beaver, their fur also made exquisite felt which was used in stovepipe hats that were the height of men's fashion in such far away places as New York and London in the early 1800's. The lure of beaver skins brought the first white men to this serene valley. With pelts bringing as much as $6.00 a piece (a small fortune at that time), many a man caught "beaver fever" and headed for the mountains to try his hand at trapping for "soft gold."

From the headwaters of the Missouri River on the north to the Great Salt Lake in the south, hundreds of hardy young men combed the mountains for beaver rich streams like this one. Whether they worked for a fur company or struck out alone as "free trappers", these colorful characters emerged as America's unrivaled frontiersmen. To some, they are remembered as braggarts, liars and rapscallions. But all in all, with little more than their wits and rifle, these remarkable men masterfully navigated rugged terrain, fought Indians, faced grizzly bear, overcame cold inhospitable conditions and blazed a path for our nation to follow. Their ranks included such illustrious men as John Colter, believed to be the first white man to view the Tetons in 1807-08; David Jackson, who's love for the valley beneath the Tetons caused his trapping partner to name it after him in 1829; Jedediah Smith, a trapper and renowned explorer who was deeply religious and carried a Bible with him throughout his journeys; and Jim Bridger, the most famous mountain man, who's tall tales are enjoyed to this day.

For over 20 years, these mountain men trapped and traded. Their midsummer "rendezvous" grew from a small gathering to cash in pelts and replenish supplies to a frontier fair, a raucous celebration attended by hundreds of trappers and numerous trading companies. Then in 1840, a change in men's haberdashery caused hats of silk to replace those of beaver, and the reign of the mountain man ended as quickly as it began.

Mountain men named the Snake River not for its serpent-like meandering through the valley, as one might expect. Rather, it was named for the Shoshone Indians, who as a result of a misinterpretation of their sign language, were known to many trappers as the Snake Indians. Like all tribes, the Shoshone had a sign to designate their Nation. Theirs was a wavering hand gesture, simulating the weaving of grass which probably intended to say in effect "we are the people of woven grass shelters."

As you walk, scan the sky for circling birds of prey like the distinctive bald eagle or the brown and white osprey. These birds nest in the large cottonwood trees which thrive in the river bottoms. The osprey, sometimes called a "fishhawk," is indeed a skillful fisherman, plunging feet first into the river to retrieve its prey. But, few can match the airborne hunting ability of the eagle. Keen eyesight is used to spot favorite foods such as fish, ducks and small rodents. Then with great skill, it folds its wings and swoops in for the kill. Eagles have also been known to bully ospreys into dropping their catch, then nab it in mid-air.

Keep a sharp eye out for other animals as well. This is good country for spotting elk, mule deer, antelope and even buffalo. Droppings from the buffalo, which resemble cowpatties, are commonly seen in this area. Indians and early settlers used "buffalo chips" as fuel for fires. If you see a buffalo, give it a wide berth. The male usually weighs a ton or more and is considered the largest land mammal in North America. Both the male and the female have horns which are made of compacted hair around a bony core. Horns are permanent features and are not shed annually like antlers grown by deer, elk and moose. These horns are dangerous weapons.

Coyotes are also commonly seen in this area of the park. This very adaptive predator plays an important role in nature's ecosystem. While they eat anything from insects to an elk carcass, they prey primarily on small rodents. As hunters, they depend on their acute senses, exceptional speed (40 mph) and leaping ability (10 feet). These cunning animals rival a cat in stalking ability.

About 1/2 mile from the trailhead, the channel bends to the left toward the mountains and a third beaver dam, together with an old beaver lodge, can be seen. The trail dissipates here and it is recommended that you make this your turn around point.

④ RENDEZVOUS MOUNTAIN

Vegetation struggles to survive on Rendezvous Mountain.

TRAILHEAD: This short hike begins and ends at the top of the aerial tram at the Jackson Hole Ski Area, 21 miles from the town of Jackson, Wyoming. From Jackson, take Highway 22 west (toward Teton Pass), turn right on the Teton Village Road and follow the signs to the ski area. A large, double reversible tram will take you to the top of Rendezvous Mountain (10,450'). There is a charge for the tram which typically operates 8 a.m. to 7 p.m. during peak summer season. (GPS @ base of tram: 43° 35' 17" N, 110° 49' 39" W)

DISTANCE: 1.2 miles (round-trip).

ELEVATION CHANGES: 530 foot drop and return climb (the tram carries you the other 4,100 feet).

TIME REQUIRED: 1 hour (plus tram rides).

DIFFICULTY: Moderate.

COMMENTS: The aerial tram transports you effortlessly to the top of Rendezvous Mountain where you'll enjoy spectacular views of Jackson Hole and can explore the fascinating alpine tundra. At 10,000 feet, air pressure is low and your body gets a third less oxygen than at sea level. Take care not to overexert. It's also a good idea to take along a jacket or wind-breaker on this trip.

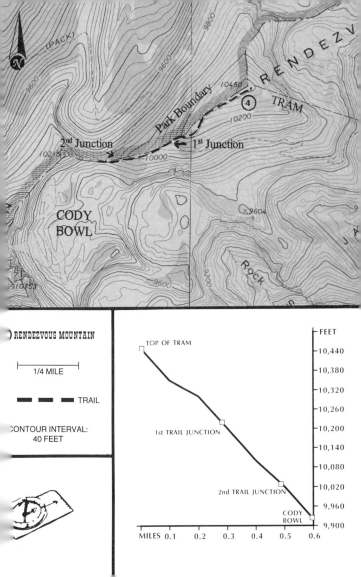

(PACK)

RENDEZV

Park Boundary

10450

④ TRAM

10200

2nd Junction

1st Junction

10245

10000

CODY
BOWL

X 9604

Rock

9200

9600

10753

RENDEZVOUS MOUNTAIN

1/4 MILE

TRAIL

CONTOUR INTERVAL:
40 FEET

TOP OF TRAM

FEET

10,440

10,380

10,320

10,260

10,200

1st TRAIL JUNCTION

10,140

10,080

10,020

2nd TRAIL JUNCTION

9,960

CODY
BOWL

9,900

MILES 0.1   0.2   0.3   0.4   0.5   0.6

The Jackson Hole Ski Area, which opened in 1965, boasts the highest vertical rise of any ski area in America. As the tram ascends, notice the service road which snakes up the mountain. This 7.2 mile route is used for the annual end of the summer run to the top of Rendezvous Mountain. Such runs are great sport in this part of the country and are vigorously trained for. In 1991 Mr. Rob Weed made it to the top in an amazing 1 hour and 2 minutes!

As you disembark the tram, you quickly realize it has transported you into a different world—the biotic community known as alpine tundra, which exists in the lofty heights along the top of the Teton Range. The climate is cool and moist and often windy. The soil is scant and supports a sparse population of dwarf trees, shrubs and flowers. Although it appears barren at first, Rendezvous Mountain is actually home to many animals. The Audubon Society has identified over 80 species of birds in the area, including golden eagle, prairie falcon, cliff swallow, Clark's nutcracker, and mountain bluebird. Also present are golden mantled ground squirrels, pikas, snowshoe hare and yellowbellied marmots.

After you have soaked up the scenery from the top of the mountain, it's time to do a little exploring. Follow the well-beaten path which leads southwest toward "Cody Bowl." Along the way look closely at the dwarfed whitebark pine trees in the area. They are known as "krummholz" trees, a German term meaning "crooked wood." Notice how the strong, prevailing southwest winds have caused the branches to grow much longer on the northeast side of the trees. The height of these trees tell us the depth of the winter snows. The extreme winter conditions kill any sprouts which protrude above the snow's insulation. Although these dwarfed trees may grow to be hundreds of years old, they are considered adolescents because under these conditions they do not develop reproductive tissues. So how did they get here you ask? Its thanks to the Clark's nutcracker, which feeds on whitebark seeds found at lower elevations. In the fall, the nutcracker collects up to 100 seeds in its sublingual pouch before flying to open areas like this to hide them in the ground. It may dine on the cached seeds throughout the winter. Although these birds have an uncanny ability to relocate the seeds, many are left behind. Only a few of these will survive to grow into trees. But, with a life span of up to 400 years, it does not take many new trees to maintain this elfin forest.

The alpine floral displays in July and August are also striking. Like the trees, the flowers which grow at this elevation must adapt to survive. They are characteristically smaller than their cousins at lower elevations and often grow in mats or cushions to avoid the wind and to trap heat. Very gently feel a mat of flowers. They can be up to 20 degrees F warmer than the surrounding air. They also bloom with more intense colors, which absorb heat better and attract insect pollinators. In this area, look for wild blue flax (a five petaled single flower on top of a slender stem), silky phacelia (foot-high stems covered with feathery purple flowers), yellow sulpher paintbrush (an obvious cousin to the red Indian paintbrush), shrubby cinquefoil (which resembles a small yellow wild rose), intricate yellow columbine (with 5 petals and 4 prominent hollow spurs which extend backward) and many flowered phlox (a ground-hugging mat of tiny white flowers).

After .3 miles, and a drop of 250 feet in elevation, the trail to Cody Bowl forks to the right. Shortly thereafter, you will come to a large rock of Darby Dolomite, a dark brown sedimentary formation made of deposits which settled to the bottom of an ancient turbid sea. The unusual plant which makes its home in this rock is called the "rock breaker." That's exactly what it is doing as it extends its roots further and further into the crack. Notice also the black, white and orange patches of color you see on this rock. These are lichens—a combination of fungus and algae living and growing together in a symbiotic relationship. Conditions are such that neither could exist independently of the other, but as a team they can survive. The algae uses the fungus to anchor itself to the rock while the fungus takes nourishment from the algae's photosynthesis process. There are over 10,000 combinations of lichen in the world. The three you see here are Jewel Lichen (orange), Map Lichen (white) and Stud Lichen (black). Some lichen live up to 4,500 years and attach themselves so firmly to the surface that they cannot be removed without breaking the rock.

At the .5 mile mark you reach a second trail junction. To the right is the trailhead for Marion Lake and Granite Canyon (see hike #15 in this guide for a description). You should continue straight another tenth of a mile or so to get a good look at Cody Bowl. As you look out over the vast expanse of Cody Bowl you see many layers of sedimentary rock stacked one on top of the other and all tilting back to the west as a result of the uplifting action of the massive Teton fault block. These layers of rock were deposited by intermittent inland seas over many millions of years. The appearance and physical characteristics of the rock reflect the varied environments of deposition, such as the prevailing climate or water depth at the time it was laid down. The top third of Cody Bowl is made up of Madison Limestone. A distinct line separates it from the middle third which is composed of the Darby Formation. Lower elevations of the mountain contain both Bighorn Dolomite and Gallatin Limestone.

Cody Peak is the location of some really radical skiing each winter. Several dozen people have skied down many of the ravines or "couloirs" which now have names like "Once is Enough" and "Twice is Nice." The large "Central Couloir," which begins near the highest part of Cody Bowl, contains two 30 foot jumps and is considered one of the most difficult in the area. Just thinking about it should give you the exhilaration needed to hike back to the tram.

Ordinarily, the man who loves the woods and the mountains, the trees, the flowers, and the wild things, has in him some indefinable quality of charm which appeals even to those sons of civilization who care for little outside of paved streets and brick walls.

—Teddy Roosevelt
January 1915.

Jenny Lake shuttle heads NW towards Mount St. John.

TRAILHEAD: The easiest way to reach the trailhead is via an inexpensive shuttle boat which departs from Jenny Lake's East Shore Boat Dock approximately every 20 minutes from 8 a.m. to 6 p.m. during summer months. The East Shore Boat Dock is located near Jenny Lake Ranger Station, 8 miles north of Moose Junction on the west side of the Teton Park Road. You can skip the boat and walk around Jenny Lake. However, that adds 2 miles to the hike, each way. (GPS @ East Shore Boat Dock: 43° 45' 05" N, 110° 43' 20" W)

DISTANCE: 2 miles (round-trip).

ELEVATION CHANGES: 420 feet.

TIME REQUIRED: 1.5 hours (plus boat rides).

DIFFICULTY: Moderate.

COMMENTS: This is possibly the most popular hike in the Tetons. But don't let the crowds scare you away. The combination of a pristine alpine lake, a powerful cascade, a spectacular view of Jackson Hole and a chance to get close to the towering Teton summits, makes this hike well worth your time. For additional information, you can purchase an inexpensive flier titled "Cascade Canyon Trail," at NPS Visitor Centers.

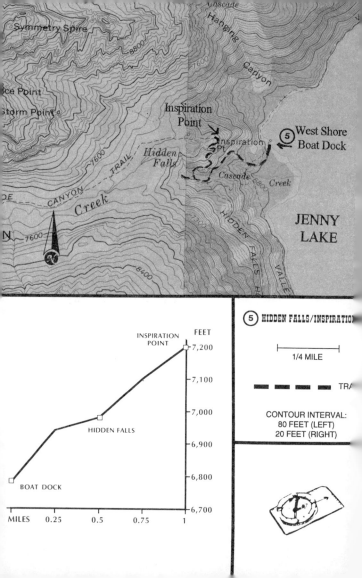

Symmetry Spire

8800

ce Point

torm Point

CANYON TRAIL

Hidden Falls

Creek

N   7600

8400

Cascade

Hanging

Canyon

7600

Inspiration Point

Inspiration Pt.

Cascade Creek

6600

HIDDEN FALLS TR.

VALLEY

⑤ West Shore Boat Dock

JENNY LAKE

7700

⑤ HIDDEN FALLS/INSPIRATIO

|—————————|
1/4 MILE

━ ━ ━ ━ ━   TRA

CONTOUR INTERVAL:
80 FEET (LEFT)
20 FEET (RIGHT)

INSPIRATION POINT

HIDDEN FALLS

BOAT DOCK

FEET
7,200
7,100
7,000
6,900
6,800
6,700

MILES   0.25   0.5   0.75   1

For many, visiting Jenny Lake is the highlight of their trip. This spectacular 326 foot deep jewel lies beneath the loftiest Teton summits. It was named by the 1872 Hayden Geological Survey in honor of Jenny Leigh, the Shoshone Indian wife of English-born "Beaver Dick" Leigh, who for decades guided prominent visitors (including Hayden) through Jackson Hole. Ironically, just four years after the naming of this beautiful lake had given Jenny a touch of immortality, her life and those of her 6 children were taken by smallpox.

As the shuttle boat departs, the highest peak directly ahead of you is Mount St. John (11,430') named for Orestes St. John, a geologist on the later 1877 Hayden Survey. To your left lies jagged-topped Teewinot Mountain (12,325'), a Shoshone Indian name meaning "many pinnacles." Between these two mountains lies Cascade Canyon, which reveals its impressive size and distinctive U- shape as the West Shore Boat Dock is neared.

From the dock, the trail to Hidden Falls turns left and begins a gradual climb through a lush spruce-fir forest. These shade-tolerant trees thrive in this moist, sheltered environment. Some of the larger spruce trees are judged to be approximately 300 years old. This is a good spot to introduce yourself to a tree. That's right, reach out and shake hands with a branch! If the single needles are square, sharp and inhospitable, you have likely met a spruce. However, if the needles are flat, flexible and friendly to the touch, you have just befriended a fir.

Many trails criss-cross this area; however, following the signs to Hidden Falls is not difficult. Along the way, notice the "Buck and Rail" fences which have come to be closely associated with the beauty of Jackson Hole. The name comes from the X-shaped supports or "crossbucks" and the "rails" attached to them. Resourceful settlers in Jackson Hole constructed fences in this manner to avoid digging post holes in the rocky soil.

The trail twice crosses Cascade Creek. Just prior to the second crossing, a short spur trail to the left leads to a photographic point at the base of Hidden Falls. Here the creek, fed by melt-water from the heavy winter snows, tumbles impressively down a steep 250-foot foaming cascade. To your left, as you view the falls, is an open boulder field known as the "practice rocks," where aspiring mountaineers learn the basics—knots, belaying and rappelling—from Exum Mountain

Guides, the oldest mountaineering school in the country. After just two days of intensive work, students are ready to test their skill on a guided climb to the top of the Grand Teton.

As you continue, the main trail crosses Cascade Creek and begins a 200 foot ascent, via several switchbacks, to your ultimate destination, Inspiration Point. This trail was skillfully cut through the rock by the Civilian Conservation Corps in the 1930's. The exposed rock in this area is principally a light-gray granite made up of fine grained crystals of gray quartz and white feldspar with few flakes of black biotite mica and white muscovite mica. Granite is an igneous rock formed from the cooling and hardening of molten magma deep beneath the earth's surface. This rock was later raised and exposed as part of the massive block fault which created the Teton Range beginning some 9 million years ago.

From Inspiration Point (7,200') Jenny Lake and much of Jackson Hole spread out at your feet. Contemplate for a moment the powerful geologic forces which combined to create the landscape before you. At the same time the Tetons were rising, this valley was dropping. The slippage between the rising mountains and the falling valley occurred (and still occurs) along the Teton Fault which follows the base of the Teton Range just beneath you. Actually, the valley has fallen much further than the mountains have risen; however, subsequently deposited glacial debris have filled in much of the valley.

Over the past 2 million years the earth's climate cycled between cold and warm periods. With each cold period came massive glaciation. Geologists have found evidence of at least 3 major glacial periods which occurred here in the last 250,000 years. The first and most extensive period saw several thousand feet thick, flowing south along the face of the Teton Range. The latest period was much less extensive. However, because it ended just 10,000 years ago, its effects on the landscape can be readily discerned. During that period a powerful glacier descended Cascade Canyon, scraping and eroding the canyon walls until they formed their current broad U-shape. The glacier spilled onto the valley floor and scooped out what is now Jenny Lake. The small tree-studded, levee-like ridge which surrounds the lake is actually a glacial moraine marking the furthest point the glacier pushed into the valley. Glacial moraines, which contain more fertile, water retaining soils, are almost without exception heavily forested. The other partial moraine which can be seen from Inspiration Point is called "Timbered Island." This small, forested ridge, surrounded by a "sea" of sagebrush, was left stranded in the valley by an earlier glacial episode.

The effects of another extremely recent geological event can be seen from Inspiration Point. As you look beyond Timbered Island to the far side of the valley, a mile long and 1/2 mile wide gash appears in the Gros Ventre (pronounced "Grow Vaunt") Mountains. This is the site of the 1925 Gros Ventre Slide, one of the largest natural earth movements in the world. Here, in just minutes, some 50 million cubic yards of limestone, shale and rock, came crashing down from the top of Sheep Mountain (11,200').

If you decide to explore further up Cascade Canyon, see the Lake Solitude hike (#13 in this guide book).

⑥ STRING AND LEIGH LAKES

Mount Moran dominates the skyline above Leigh Lake.

TRAILHEAD: The trail begins near String Lake Picnic Area. From North Jenny Lake Junction on the Teton Park Road, turn west and drive 1.5 miles on the Jenny Lake loop road. Then, turn right at the sign marked "String Lake" and proceed to the third and final parking area. A large trailhead sign marks the beginning of the trail to "Leigh Lake." (GPS: 43° 47' 13" N, 110° 43' 50" W)

DISTANCE: 4.5 miles (round-trip).

ELEVATION CHANGES: 40 Feet.

TIME REQUIRED: 2.5 hours.

DIFFICULTY: Easy.

COMMENTS: This delightful hike takes you along placid String Lake and through lodgepole pine forests on the way to beautiful Leigh Lake, the third largest in the park. It affords hikers some of the closest and most spectacular views of magnificent Mount Moran (12,605').

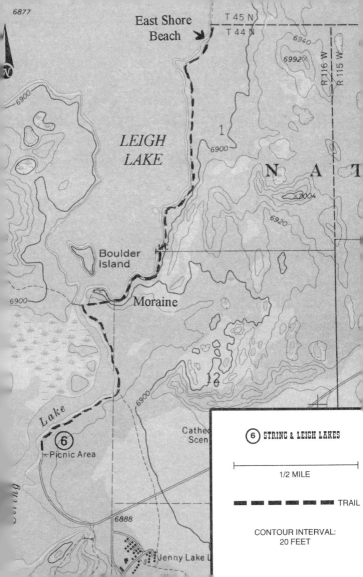

East Shore
Beach

T 45 N
T 44 N

6877

6940

6992

R 116 W
R 115 W

LEIGH
LAKE

1

6900

N A T

X 7004

6920

Boulder
Island

Moraine

6900

6900

6

6900

Lake

Cathed
Scen

Picnic Area
6

6888

Jenny Lake

6 STRING & LEIGH LAKES

1/2 MILE

TRAIL

CONTOUR INTERVAL:
20 FEET

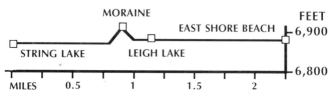

The first .9 miles of this trail follow the eastern shoreline of aptly named String Lake, a shallow, narrow body of water which connects Leigh Lake with Jenny Lake. In the summer, String Lake is a popular spot for swimming, picnicking and canoeing. On the opposite side of the lake the Tetons begin their dramatic mile high rise from the valley floor. Until relatively recent geologic time there were no mountains here. Then, about 9 million years ago, the earth's crust began to slip and break into the separate blocks on either side of what is now called the Teton Fault. The western block rose to form the Teton Range while the eastern block dropped dramatically to form the valley. Actually, the valley block fell far more than the mountain block rose. However, subsequently deposited glacial debris have filled in much of the valley. This section of the trail closely parallels the Teton Fault. In fact, geologists have found fairly recent fault scraps on the west side of String Lake which clearly indicate that the mountains are still rising and the valley is still falling.

The falling valley is like a giant trap door hinged along the highlands on the eastern side of Jackson Hole. Therefore, the greatest drop in the valley occurred, and is still occurring, right here on its western edge. Thus, unlike normal valleys which slope inward toward a central river, Jackson Hole tilts westward toward the Tetons. Streams flowing out of the Tetons in this area do not travel directly east to the Snake River. Instead, they turn almost immediately to the south and flow from Leigh, String and Jenny lakes out through Cottonwood Creek, which eventually joins the Snake farther down-river.

Just before reaching Leigh Lake you will pass several trail junctions. You should continue to the right along the "Leigh Lake Trail" which leads another 1.4 miles to the sandy East Shore Beach. To reach Leigh Lake, the trail traverses a small 20 foot, levee-like ridge. This is actually a moraine left behind some 15,000 years ago by glaciers which flowed out of Leigh and Paintbrush canyons and spilled onto the valley floor. This moraine, which today surrounds and contains Leigh Lake, marks the furthest point these combined glaciers proceeded into the valley.

Leigh Lake, the third largest in the park, is two miles long and 250 feet deep. It is named for "Beaver Dick" Leigh, a trapper, hunter and guide. From the 1860's until his death in 1899, he guided many a prominent party through this territory, including the 1872 Hayden Geological Survey and an 1892 hunting party which included Teddy Roosevelt. Ferdinand Hayden so appreciated his guide that he named Leigh Lake after him and Jenny Lake after his Shoshone Indian wife. Tragically, this wild country took its toll on the Leigh family. In 1876, smallpox took the life of his wife, Jenny, and their six small children as he stood helplessly by.

An imposing flat-topped, glacier-draped mountain towers nearly 6,000 feet above Leigh Lake to the west. Early Indians called it "the mountain of the square shoulders." Hayden named it Mount Moran after Thomas Moran, the prominent landscape painter who participated in several of the Hayden surveys. The mountain is made up primarily of hard Precambrian basement rocks, including Layered Gneiss (pronounced "nice") and Granite Gneiss. However, the top 50 feet which cap the mountain are comprised of relatively younger Flathead Sandstone, a type of sedimentary rock which formed along the shoreline of vast inland seas that existed here over 500 million years ago. Long before the Teton uplift, over millions of years, many layers of sedimentary rocks were deposited, forming an unbroken horizontal blanket covering the basement rocks beneath. As the mountains rose and the valley fell, the sedimentary rock cracked, separated and traveled great distances—the western portion rising and the eastern portion falling. Geologists have speculated that Flathead Sandstone, identical to that on top of Mount Moran, may be buried at depths of nearly 24,000 feet beneath the floor of Jackson Hole. If that is the case, the slippage along the Teton Fault would be some 30,000 vertical feet.

Five of the twelve active glaciers in the park adorn the slopes of Mount Moran. The glacier easily spotted from Leigh Lake is known as "Falling Ice Glacier." Also readily noticeable is the 150-foot-wide, black, ribbon-like column cutting vertically through the face of the mountain. This distinctive geological feature is a "dike," formed when molten magma welled up into a fissure in the older Precambrian rock. When the magma cooled, it formed a dark-colored, low-silica rock known as "diabase." This diabase dike extends from a point near the far shore of Leigh Lake, up through the face of Mount Moran and has been traced westward more than seven miles.

The dominant tree seen along this trail is the lodgepole pine. This tall, straight, slender tree was commonly used by Indians in constructing their lodges, hence the name "lodgepole." Because these trees have no center tap root, southwest winds whipping across Leigh Lake have toppled many a mature tree. This is one way nature maintains her delicate balance. The fallen trees slowly rot, returning vital nutrients to the soil. In the meantime, they provide a home for many insects and small animals, which in turn attract larger animals that feed on them. Listen for the chatter of the red squirrel and watch for his quick darting moves. Although they appear playful, they must be constantly vigilant to elude the crafty pine marten, also living here. This long, sleek, short-legged animal with a tiny fox-like face and brown bushy tail is a formidable predator, feeding principally on small rodents. Another inhabitant is the porcupine. Unlike the squirrel, its survival does not depend on speed and quick wits. Their sharp quills make them a living fortress. Did you know they are born with those quills? Fortunately for the mother, the quills do not harden and become dangerous until shortly after birth.

At the 2.2 mile mark you reach the lovely white sands of Leigh Lake's East Shore Beach. Virtually all the other lakes in the park are surrounded by rocks and gravel. But, here on the windward side of Leigh Lake, the winds build as they cross the length of the lake. On most afternoons, the waves pound the shore and provide insight as to how this beautiful beach came to exist. This is an excellent spot to rest before turning around.

As you return to the trailhead, look for wild huckleberries, a two to three-foot high bushy shrub bearing a plethora of delicious reddish-purple berries, and for grouse whortleberries, a six to eight-inch high light green shrub with tiny egg-shaped leaves and minute, but flavorful red berries. These berries ripen in late summer. It is legal to pick them. So, if you are confident in your identification, munching on a few berries is a great way to conclude your trip.

⑦ TAGGART AND BRADLEY LAKES

Forest fire leads to more diverse communities of life.

TRAILHEAD: Begin at the Taggart Trail Parking Area located 3.5 miles north of Moose Junction and 5 miles south of South Jenny Lake Junction on the west side of the Teton Park Road. (GPS: 43° 41' 37" N, 110° 43' 53" W)

DISTANCE: 5 miles (round-trip).

ELEVATION CHANGES: The trail makes three short climbs of 300, 250 and 100 feet, respectively.

TIME REQUIRED: 3 hours.

DIFFICULTY: Moderate.

COMMENTS: This is the best hike in Grand Teton National Park to view and understand the effects of forest fire on an environment. For additional information, you may wish to purchase an inexpensive brochure titled "Taggart Lake Trail," available at NPS Visitor Centers.

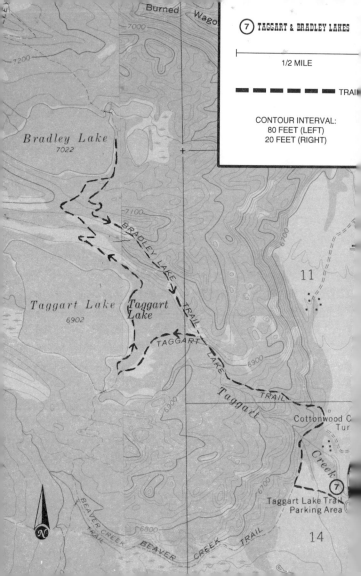

7 TAGGART & BRADLEY LAKES

|————————————————| 1/2 MILE

━━ ━━ ━━ ━━ ━━ TRAIL

CONTOUR INTERVAL:
80 FEET (LEFT)
20 FEET (RIGHT)

Burned Wago

7000

7200

Bradley Lake
7022

7100

BRADLEY LAKE TRAIL

Taggart Lake
6902

Taggart Lake

TAGGART

LAKE

TAGGART

6900

6700

11

6900

Taggart

TRAIL

Cottonwood C
Tur

Creek

7

Taggart Lake Trail
Parking Area

14

6700

BEAVER CREEK TRAIL

BEAVER   CREEK   TRAIL

6900

N

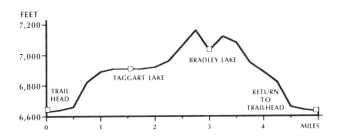

The first .2 miles of the trail lead west toward the high peaks of the Teton Range. As you cross the flat dry terrain, look closely at the ground's surface. You will find sand and a few smooth pebbles, but very little topsoil. You are walking across an ancient riverbed over 10,000 years old. Numerous streams, fed by meltwater from receding glaciers, stripped away the topsoil and left behind the sand and gravel still present today.

At the first trail junction turn right and follow the shorter route to Taggart Lake. In August of 1985, a lightning-caused forest fire ripped through this area, burning over 1,000 acres before it was contained. Although it is hard for many visitors to accept, these changes are neither good nor bad. Rather, they are simply an inevitable part of nature's constantly changing ecosystem. Ironically, the death and destruction of one forest provides the best conditions for the birth of a new, more diverse forest.

Soon the trail crosses over several channels of Taggart Creek and enters an area thick with young aspen trees. Here, aspens rarely reproduce through seeds. Instead, new trees sprout from the roots of other trees. That's why aspens usually grow in clusters and in the fall the leaves of interconnected "clone" trees simultaneously turn to gold. Aspen trees are pioneers, one of the first plants to take hold following a forest fire and begin the process of regeneration. Somehow fire stimulates the rootsystems of burned aspens, causing a much greater production of small "sucker" trees like you see thriving in this area.

43

As the trail begins to climb, search for other changes brought on by the fire. Just about everything was effected in some way, even the rocks! Take a closer look at one or more of the large granite boulders which glaciers left strewn about this area many thousands of years ago. As a result of the intense heat from the fire, tiny crystallite minerals at or near the surface of these rocks expanded, causing good-sized slabs of rock to crack and chip and break away from the cooler core. Seeing this helps us understand that the earth is constantly changing. Over millions of years, mountains are built, then torn down, only to be rebuilt again. These changes are difficult to comprehend because they happen so slowly. The Tetons began rising some 10 million years ago; since that time many glaciers have carved and eroded the peaks and have brought large chunks of granite, like these, down into the valley. Now, the forest fire has advanced the continuous natural erosion process. Over time, many such events will eventually decompose these boulders, and even the Tetons themselves, as the earth continues its never-ending cycle of change.

Most of the charred trees you see along the trail were lodgepole pine. Some of these "ghost trees" will remain standing for decades. This is longer than they would stand in a more humid climate that would better support the growth of fungi and bacteria that rot trees. Although they may appear ugly to some, it is important to remember that there are more than just trees in a forest. It is a complex life system which includes: trees and shrubs; flowers and grasses; large and small animals; lakes and streams; soils and minerals; insects and birds; etc. Each is interdependent on, and in competition with, the other. For example, fire has killed these trees but the nutrients which were locked up in them have been turned to ash and released into the soil, giving it a surge of energy and causing many new plants to grow such as snowbrush, chokecherries and birchleaf spirea. It is kind of like nature's "chemlawn." These nutrients also found their way into Taggart Creek, possibly enriching the aquatic systems to the advantage of the fish population. In addition, the fire burned off the forest canopy allowing more light to reach the forest floor, again encouraging new growth and making creatures on the ground temporarily more vulnerable to airborne predators.

At the 1.1 mile mark a second trail junction is reached. You should turn left and continue another half mile to Taggart Lake. Along the way you will see how the lodgepole forest also is regenerating itself. There is a plethora of young lodgepoles growing in this area, all fairly uniform in height, which seeded as a result of the fire. The lodgepole pine actually has two types of seed cones. In addition to their biennial cones, they produce a special "serotinous cone," which only opens at temperatures exceeding 113 degrees F. These cones may stay on the tree for twenty years or more, waiting for a forest fire to trigger the release of their seeds. Studies have shown that lodgepole forests can produce up to 1,000,000 seeds per acre following a fire. No wonder there are so many young trees growing here!

> ... *Now a flood of fire, now a flood of ice, now a flood of water and again in the fullness of time an outburst of organic life.*
> —John Muir

At the 1.6 mile mark Taggart Lake is reached. Across the lake you get an excellent view up Avalanche Canyon. On the left side of the broad U-shaped canyon lies Mount Wister (11,490'), named for Owen Wister, author of The Virginian, a turn of the century novel set in the Tetons, which made famous the expression "When you call me that, smile!" The right side of the canyon is dominated by Nez Perce Peak (11,901'), named in honor of the proud Indian tribe which traveled this part of the Rocky Mountains. The Nez Perce (French for "pierced nose") are most often remembered for their skillful and valiant 1877 fighting retreat from the U.S. Cavalry. Driven to warfare by the pressure of land greed, they made a 1,300 mile flight across the west in a failed attempt to reach Canada and safety.

Avalanche Canyon, Taggart Lake and the hill you just climbed owe their existence to relatively recent glacial action. During the "pinedale glaciation," which ended just over 10,000 years ago, a powerful glacier flowed out of Avalanche Canyon and spread onto the valley floor. Over many thousands of years, it carved the canyon, scooped out the hollow now occupied by Taggart Lake and built up the 300 foot moraine which completely encircles the lake and outlines the furthest point of glacial advance.

From the trail junction at Taggart Lake, you should turn right and continue along the lake shore, climb up and over another glacial moraine and drop down to glacier scooped Bradley Lake which lies 1.4 miles away. Both of these beautiful lakes were named by members of the 1872 Hayden Survey. Frank Bradley and W.R. Taggart were geologists on the expedition. Other Hayden Survey members who were given a bit of immortality were guide "Beaver Dick" Leigh (Leigh Lake) and his wife Jenny (Jenny Lake), and Artist Thomas Moran (Mount Moran), just to name a few. The leader of these surveys and numerous other expeditions throughout the Rocky Mountains was Ferdinand V. Hayden, an army surgeon turned geologist who's energy and voraciousness caused the Indians he encountered to dub him "the man-who-picks-up-stones-running."

For the final leg of this loop hike, return to the trail junction which you passed on the south side of Bradley Lake, veer to the left and proceed 2 miles to the trailhead. As you climb, watch for wild huckleberries. This three- foot high bushy shrub bears a plethora of delicious reddish-purple berries beginning in August. It is legal to pick berries in national parks. So, if you are confident in your identification, munching on a few sweet juicy berries is a great way to conclude your trip.

> ... *Few* such [mountains] stand among so broad, deep valleys as to give so great relative elevations and to be seen so prominently . . . . This must become a favorite for tourists.
>
> —Ferdinand V. Hayden
> *Notes on the Tetons and Jackson Hole,* 1872.

⑧ HERMITAGE POINT

The placid beauty of lily pad-covered Heron Pond.

TRAILHEAD: The trail begins near Colter Bay Marina, situated on the east side of Jackson Lake, 5.5 miles north of Jackson Lake Junction on U.S. Highway 89/191. To reach the trailhead, take the Colter Bay Village turn-off and follow the road all the way to the end. Then, turn left and continue to the far south side of the marina parking lot, where you will see the "Hermitage Point Trailhead" sign. (GPS: 43° 54' 03" N, 110° 38' 28" W)

DISTANCE: 9.5 miles (round-trip).

ELEVATION CHANGES: The trail is mostly flat, but contains several short climbs of less than 100 feet.

TIME REQUIRED: 5 hours.

DIFFICULTY: Moderate.

COMMENTS: The extensive trail network in this area is confusing. The suggested route to Hermitage Point runs counter clockwise, passing Heron Pond on the way out and Swan Lake on the way back. Review the map carefully before departing and consult it as necessary.

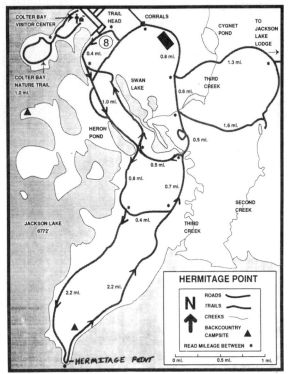

COLTER BAY
VISITOR CENTER

TRAIL
HEAD

CORRALS

CYGNET
POND

TO
JACKSON
LAKE
LODGE →

8

0.4 mi.

0.8 mi.

1.3 mi.

COLTER BAY
NATURE TRAIL
1.0 mi.

SWAN
LAKE

THIRD
CREEK

1.0 mi.

0.6 mi.

HERON
POND

0.5 mi.

1.6 mi.

0.5 mi.

0.8 mi.

0.7 mi.

SECOND
CREEK

JACKSON LAKE
6772'

0.4 mi.

THIRD
CREEK

2.2 mi.

2.2 mi.

HERMITAGE POINT

HERMITAGE POINT

N

— ROADS
TRAILS
CREEKS
▲ BACKCOUNTRY
CAMPSITE
READ MILEAGE BETWEEN *

0 mi.   0.5 mi.   1 mi.

Map courtesy of Grand Teton National History Association.

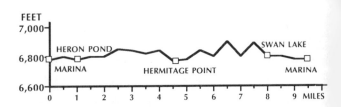

FEET
7,000

HERON POND

SWAN LAKE

6,800

MARINA

HERMITAGE POINT

MARINA

6,600

0   1   2   3   4   5   6   7   8   9 MILES

From the trailhead marker, follow the path marked "foot trail" to the right as it passes a gate and continues along the Colter Bay Marina. Colter Bay was named in honor of John Colter, believed to be the first white man to lay eyes on the Tetons. He journeyed west as a member of the 1804-1806 Lewis and Clark expedition, then decided to stay. Colter was given permission to leave the home-bound expedition, according to Lewis and Clark's journals, because "we were disposed to be of service to anyone of our party who had performed their duty as well as Colter." After assisting in the establishment of a trading post at the confluence of the Yellowstone and Bighorn rivers, Colter, in the winter of 1807-1808, set out to spread the word to the Crow Indian Nation that they could trade their pelts for blankets, beads and tobacco. It was on this remarkable trek that Colter is believed to have visited what is today Grand Teton and Yellowstone national parks.

After .4 miles, take a right at the first trail junction and head for Heron Pond. Skip the detour to "Jackson Lake Overlook;" the intermittent views are not worth the 150 foot climb. At the one mile mark, the north end of Heron Pond is reached. It's delicate beauty is primarily due to the numerous Rocky Mountain pond lilies which thrive in the shallow waters. This attractive plant is well adapted to its aquatic habitat. The "lily pads" are unique in that the stomata, openings through which the plant breathes, are located on top of the leaf so that the water does not restrict the necessary passage of oxygen and carbon dioxide. In addition, the long root stalks anchoring the plant to the muddy bottom are coated in a slimy mucus, which prevents them from sawing each other in half as they sway back and forth in water.

As you pass Heron Pond keep a sharp eye out for moose. These curious looking creatures are also highly specialized for aquatic life. Their long legs allow them to move freely about in marshy areas, their body secretes an oil which makes their coat more water repellent and they actually have hollow hair, which makes them more buoyant swimmers. This is also a good area to spot a variety of waterfowl, including mallards with their bright green heads, Barrow's golden eye, the familiar Canada geese, or with a little luck the pond's namesake, the great blue heron. The heron is a magnificent bird standing over four feet tall. Watch for them stalking fish. They draw their long neck back in a S-shape and patiently wait for the perfect moment to strike.

At the 1.4 mile mark another trail junction is reached. Bear right and follow the path marked "Hermitage Point 3 miles" as it continues around the southern end of Heron Pond. At the 2.2 mile mark, take another right at the next junction and climb a small hill. Near the top of the hill you will notice a number of Douglas fir trees which are much larger than the lodgepole pine trees you have been seeing. The most distinctive feature of the Douglas fir is its female cone, which contains three-pronged, feather-like bracts between its scales. As you continue through the forest, look for a light green shrub about 8-10 inches high with tiny egg-shaped leaves and minute red berries. These grouse whortleberries, which ripen in August, are extremely flavorful for their size. They are terrific in muffins and pancakes or simply for munching along the trail.

Near Hermitage Point the trees turn to sagebrush and the views of the Teton Range become even more spectacular. From the point itself, Mount Moran (12,605') dominates the western sky. This distinctive flat-topped mountain is named for Thomas Moran, the famous land-scape artist whose many sketches and watercolors brought much notoriety to the Yellowstone-Grand Teton area in the 1870s. Five of the twelve active glaciers in the park adorn the slopes of Mount Moran. The peculiar shaped glacier, easily seen from this vantage, is appropriately named "Skillet Glacier." In 1950 a DC-3 airplane careened into the mountain ridge just to the right of the glacier at an elevation about level with the lower end of the skillet's handle. None of the passengers survived. Parts of the wreckage, however, remain to this day.

From Hermitage Point, this loop trail bends back to the north and briefly parallels the lake shore. The splendid backcountry campsite which is passed along the way is reminiscent of the first summer encampments made by prehistoric man on this same lake shortly after the last glaciers receded some 15,000 years ago. Over 100 archeological sites which surround Jackson Lake have produced artifacts and other clues to the lives of these nomadic hunter-gatherers. Also visible from this section of the trail is the broad silhouette of Signal Mountain and Jackson Lake Dam just to its left. The first dam on this site was constructed by the Bureau of Reclamation in 1916 and raised the lake 39 feet above its natural level.

The trail bends to the left and eventually leaves Jackson Lake behind. Continue straight at the 6.6 mile mark as another trail joins from the left. Then, at the next junction (7.3 mile mark), make a sharp left and return to Heron Pond. From the trail junction at Heron Pond (7.8 mile mark), turn right and head for Swan Lake. Beaver are principally responsible for the existence of Swan Lake. You can see one of their many dams in this area by making a short spur to your right as you reach the lake. As you continue north along the lake shore, you may be lucky enough to see one of the rare trumpeter swans which give the lake its name. A pair have been attempting to nest on the small island in the middle of the lake next to a beaver lodge. These graceful birds grow to thirty pounds and have a wingspan of eight feet. Watch for their long neck to pop up like a periscope. If you see one, there is a good chance you will see another. They often mate for life and are usually seen in pairs.

Like Heron Pond, Swan Lake is covered with water lilies. They are particularly thick on the north end of the lake. Nature is slowly converting these lakes to meadows through a process called "eutrophication". Over time, these lilies, together with other vegetation and debris washed in by streams, will gradually fill up the lake bottom. Trees and shrubs will encroach from the sides and eventually the lake will be no more. As you leave Swan Lake behind, its just a short .6 miles back to the trailhead.

The most beautiful country in the world.

—Teddy Roosevelt on The Tetons

⑨ DEATH CANYON

Passing through the "portal" to upper Death Canyon.

TRAILHEAD: The trail begins near the White Grass Ranger Station. To reach the trailhead, drive 3 miles south of the Moose Visitor Center on the Moose-Wilson Road, turn west onto the spur-road marked "Death Canyon Trailhead" and proceed 1.6 miles along a dirt road to a parking area. (GPS: 43° 39' 19" N, 110° 46' 49" W)

DISTANCE: 8 miles (round-trip).

ELEVATION CHANGES: The trail rises 400 feet, then drops 400 feet, before making a fairly strenuous 1,050 climb into to the mouth of Death Canyon.

TIME REQUIRED: 5 hours.

DIFFICULTY: Strenuous.

COMMENTS: This hike takes you up and over Phelps Lake Overlook, then climbs 1,000 feet up and through a narrow portal into a portion of the serenely beautiful upper Death Canyon. Along the way, you are treated to one of the most extraordinary rock displays in the park.

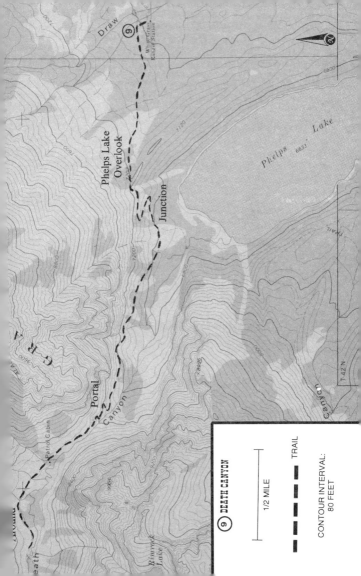

Draw

⑨

Wigwams
Ranger Station

Phelps Lake Overlook

Phelps Lake 6633'

Junction

Portal Canyon

Patrol Cabin

Canyon

Death

Bimrock Lake

T. 42 N

⑨ **DEATH CANYON**

1/2 MILE

TRAIL

CONTOUR INTERVAL:
80 FEET

DEATH CANYON

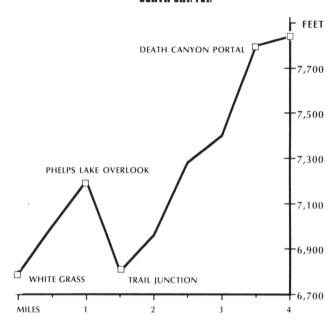

This hike initially follows the "Valley Trail" .9 miles to the top of Phelps Lake Overlook. Along the way, it passes through a forest of mostly tall slender lodgepole pine trees with intermittent subalpine fir and Engelmann spruce. The fir trees can be distinguished from the spruce by their flat flexible needles and erect cones. The spruce has sharp needles and short cones which hang down. The most prominent flowers along this section of the trail are thimbleberry, with its large red raspberry-like top, and well named monkshood, with its distinctive purple flowers which on close scrutiny form an irregular hood-shaped structure. These moisture loving plants are found here because just above the trail, a number of springs rise through a fissure formed by the Teton fault zone which runs along the base of the range.

Phelps Lake Overlook affords terrific views of the park's fourth largest lake (525 acres) and the imposing mouth of Death Canyon. The lake, the canyon and even the overlook itself owe their existence to relatively recent glacial action. During the "pinedale glaciation" period, which ended just over 10,000 years ago, a powerful glacier flowed out of Death Canyon and spread onto the valley floor. Over many thousands of years, it carved the canyon, scooped out the hollow now occupied by Phelps Lake and built up this 500 foot high lateral moraine upon which you are standing.

As you drop down the moraine to near lake level notice how the vegetation has changed. Southern facing slopes like this are exposed to the full force of the summer sun and desiccating southwesterly winds. Mountain ash and aspen trees, along with low growth sage, Oregon grape and chokeberry bushes thrive in these dry hillside environments.

At the 1.6 mile mark, take a right at the trail junction and follow the Death Canyon trail as it switchbacks up over 1,000 feet to the narrow portal which marks the entrance to the main portion of Death Canyon. This part of the trail takes you through one of the most fascinating and spectacular rock displays in the park. All along the trail are superb specimens of a rock formation known as Layered Gneiss (pronounced "nice"). These rocks are over 2.5 billion years old, placing them among the oldest rocks in North America. They are also called "basement" rocks, because they form much of the very foundation of the continent. They are composed principally of light-colored quartz and feldspar and of darker biotite mica and hornblende. The distinct black-and-white layers are made up of different proportions of these minerals. These rocks reformed some 5-to-10 miles beneath the surface under extreme pressure and temperatures exceeding 1000 degrees F. Under such conditions, the rock became soft and taffy-like. In this plastic condition, the rock folded and bent into the unusual formations readily seen along the trail. These "metamorphic rocks" (as distinguished from "igneous rocks" formed by the solidification of molten material and "sedimentary rocks" formed through the consolidation of layers of fragmental material deposited by water or air) were raised to the surface partly as a result of the Teton uplift and were further exposed by glacial erosion.

Granite, which forms the tops of many of the highest peaks in the Teton Range, is composed of the same four basic minerals found in gneiss. The difference lies in the proportion of the minerals and how the two different rocks were formed. It's like baking a cake. All cakes contain eggs, flour, milk and sugar, but the kind of cake you end up with depends on how you mix it and cook it. Granite is an igneous rock formed from the cooling and hardening of molten magma deep below the earth's surface. This process allows the minerals time to crystalize, giving it a coarse grainy texture. Because it is made up of roughly 30% quartz, 60-70% feldspar and just a smattering of darker mica and hornblende, granite has an overall light-gray color with a peppering of black.

No one is quite sure how Death Canyon got its name. One possible explanation revolves around a rumor that a member of a turn-of-the-century survey party disappeared while working in the canyon. As you continue to climb, notice the striking V-shape made by the canyon walls ahead of you. This not only makes for dramatic scenery, but also poses another mystery. As we have already discovered, the existence of Phelps Lake and the moraine which surrounds it are conclusive evidence that a large glacier once flowed out of Death Canyon. However, glaciers carve out broad U-shaped canyons, not V-shaped ones, which are associated with river erosion. So how did this narrow V-cut get in the middle of this otherwise classic example of a glacier-carved canyon? Some geologists have speculated that the hard metamorphic rock in the area may have resisted or avoided the erosive force of the glacier when it was active. Then, as the glacier receded up the canyon, the tremendous volume of glacial meltwater which churned through this area for many thousands of years cut the distinctive V-shape we see today.

At the 3.5 mile mark, the trail levels out and spectacular views of the upper canyon briefly open up. The stream moves more slowly here and willows abound. This is excellent moose habitat. It is worth the effort to continue another half-mile, to the point where the Death Canyon trail crosses the creek, before you turn around. Along the way you will pass a NPS cabin (and a trail junction) and a beautiful cascade which flows out of Rimrock Lake high above you on the left. The return hike down Death Canyon affords impressive views of Phelps Lake and of Sheep Mountain (11,200') in the Gros Ventre Range on the far side of Jackson Hole.

⑩ HANGING CANYON

Lake of the Crags nestled beneath square-topped Rock of Ages.

TRAILHEAD: The easiest way to reach the trailhead is via an inexpensive shuttle boat which departs from Jenny Lake's East Shore Boat Dock approximately every 20 minutes from 8 a.m. to 6 p.m. during summer months. The East Shore Boat Dock is located near Jenny Lake Ranger Station, 8 miles north of Moose Junction on the west side of the Teton Park Road. You can skip the boat and walk around Jenny Lake. However, that adds 2 miles to the hike, each way. (GPS @ East Shore Boat Dock: 43° 45' 05" N, 110° 43' 20" W)

DISTANCE: 6 miles (round-trip).

ELEVATION CHANGES: A very difficult 2,800 foot climb.

TIME REQUIRED: 5 hours (plus boat rides).

DIFFICULTY: Very strenuous.

COMMENTS: Hanging Canyon should be attempted by experienced hikers only. It is a very steep and potentially treacherous hike, much of which is beyond established trails. The unmarked, little maintained path is at times difficult to follow and should not be taken before the snows melt in early July. To reach Lake of the Crags, you must use a topo map and carefully follow the trail descriptions in this guide.

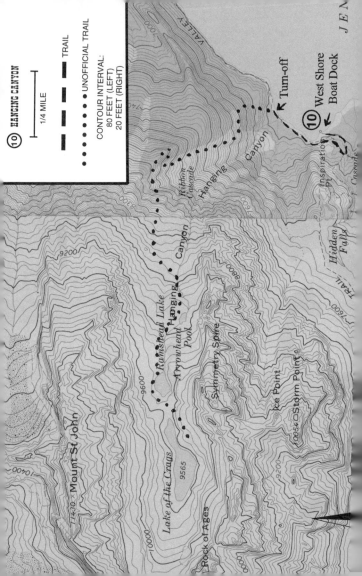

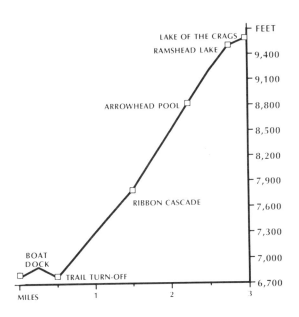

Jenny Lake, the second largest in the park, was named by the 1872 Hayden Geological Survey in honor of Jenny Leigh, the Shoshone Indian wife of "Beaver Dick" Leigh who guided the survey through the Teton region. As the shuttle boat departs, jagged-topped Teewinot Mountain (12,325'), which derives its name from the Shoshone Indian word meaning "many pinnacles," lies immediately to your left. As you look ahead, you next see Cascade Canyon, a deep glacier-carved valley, then a number of small peaks—Storm Point (10,054'), Ice Point (9,920'), Symmetry Spire (10,560') and a mile-long ridge of peaks (11,430') named after Orestes St. John, a geologist on the 1877 Hayden Survey. The entrance to Hanging Canyon actually lies two thousand feet above Jenny Lake between Symmetry Spire and Mount St. John.

From the West Shore Boat Dock, the trail turns left and begins a gradual climb through a lush spruce-fir forest, made up primarily of Engelmann spruce and subalpine fir. These shade-tolerant trees thrive in this moist, sheltered environment. The cones of the Engelmann spruce hang down, while the subalpine fir holds its purplish-colored cones upright. The most distinctive feature of the Douglas fir tree, also present here, is its female cone, which contains three-pronged, feather-like bracts between its scales.

Two-tenths of a mile from the boat dock, turn right at the junction and follow the route marked "String Lake Trail." It takes you back down near the lake, passes a junction with the Cascade Canyon Horse Trail and, about .5 miles from the dock, enters a series of small foot bridges which cross the stream that flows out of Hanging Canyon. Immediately after crossing the fourth small bridge, you should turn left and follow an unmarked, but well used path which leads to Hanging Canyon.

The path climbs through intermittent forest, then breaks into the open and affords excellent views of Ribbon Cascade ahead of you and Jenny Lake behind you. Up Cascade Canyon to your left, you see the "Cathedral Group" of peaks- -from left to right, Teewinot Mountain, Grand Teton (13,770') and Mount Owen (12,928'). It is not unusual to find natural features in America compared to old world architecture such as castles or cathedrals. To compensate for our relative lack of historical literature, architecture and art, early Americans turned to the spectacular wonders of the North American West for a scenic heritage in which to take pride.

Soon, the path bends to the right, briefly re-enters the trees, then switchbacks to the left. At this point, you have climbed 1,000 feet. As you continue to climb, Jackson Hole spreads out beneath you. In addition to Jenny Lake, you are now able to see String Lake, Jackson Lake and much of the Snake River. As you soak up the view, contemplate for a moment the powerful geologic forces which combined to create the landscape before you. As recently as 10 million years ago, there was no Teton Range. Then, the earth's crust began to slip and break into two separate blocks, moving in opposite directions. As the Tetons rose, Jackson Hole fell. The slippage between the rising mountains and falling valley occurred (and still occurs) at the Teton Fault which runs along the base of the Teton Range just beneath you. Actually the valley has fallen much further than the mountains have risen; however, subsequently deposited glacial debris and stream-laid sand and gravel have filled in much of the valley.

The route becomes steeper and more difficult to follow as it enters a series of boulder fields. Watch for small stacks of rocks which mark the way. When in doubt, continue climbing in a general westerly direction, keeping the creek on your left. Eventually the path enters the first of two ravines cut by the erosive power of the creek. At this point, you have climbed 2,000 feet. Next, you pass tiny Arrowhead Pool, which lies beneath you on the left, and follow the creek into the second ravine. Once out, it is a very short distance to beautiful Ramshead Lake, named by an early mountain climbing party who found the skull of a large bighorn sheep near the lakeshore.

From Ramshead Lake (9,500'), the rare beauty of Hanging Canyon opens up. This small, but spectacular glacier-carved canyon is surrounded by craggy peaks, the most prominent of which is square-shaped "Rock of Ages" (10,895') which lies at the head of the canyon. To its right are a number of smaller peaks with names like Schoolhouse, Canine Tooth, The Jaw, Camels Head, and Needles Eye Spire, all of which are a challenge to ambitious mountain climbers. The mouth of aptly named Hanging Canyon really does "hang" 2,000 feet above the valley floor. Such hanging valleys possibly occur as a result of smaller glaciers joining larger, deeper glaciers. Then, when both glaciers recede, the smaller glacier-cut valley is left high and dry. Fault block mountain uplift may also be a cause of hanging valleys.

It is well worth the effort to continue up the canyon to Lake of the Crags (9,565'), which lies just below Rock of Ages. Many believe it to be the most picturesque spot in all of Grand Teton National Park. As you continue through the boulder field, keep an eye out for tiny pikas (or rock rabbits) inhabiting the area. Listen for their forceful "bleats" and watch for piles of grass which they harvest and spread to dry. Once dried, the grass will be stored for winter in a den beneath the rocks.

Take time and enjoy your stay in Hanging Canyon. But, remember the last boat departs the West Shore Boat Dock at 6 p.m. Therefore, unless you are willing to hike the extra two miles, you should plan your time accordingly. Also, do not underestimate the time it will take to get back. Although it is all downhill, the boulder fields are treacherous and require as much time going down as coming up.

⑪ AMPHITHEATER LAKE

The Grand Teton viewed from the top of Surprise Lake Pinnacle.

TRAILHEAD: The trail begins at Lupine Meadows. To reach the trailhead, drive 7.5 miles north of Moose Junction or 1 mile south of South Jenny Lake Junction, on the Teton Park Road, turn west on the unpaved spur-road marked "Lupine Meadows Trailhead," and continue 1.6 miles to a parking area. (GPS: 43° 44' 05" N, 110° 44' 27" W)

DISTANCE: 11 miles (round-trip).

ELEVATION CHANGES: 3,000 feet (plus a 200-foot climb up Surprise Lake Pinnacle and 150 feet up Glacier Gulch Saddle).

TIME REQUIRED: 7 hours.

DIFFICULTY: Very strenuous.

COMMENTS: In addition to awesome mountain scenery, this strenuous hike exposes you to at least five of the 12 major biotic communities which exist in the park. As the trail ascends, the five communities explored are: sagebrush, lodgepole pine, Douglas fir, spruce-fir, and alpine tundra. Snow is a problem until midsummer.

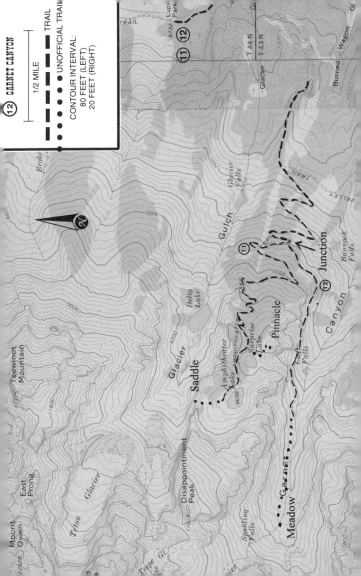

TRAIL
UNOFFICIAL TRAIL

1/2 MILE

CONTOUR INTERVAL:
80 FEET (LEFT)
20 FEET (RIGHT)

⑪ ⑫

Lupi
Park
6732

T 44 N
T 43 N

Glacier

Burned

Wagon

Gl

Broke

N

Glacier
Falls

Gulch

VALLEY TRAIL

TRAIL

⑪

Junction

Bannock
Falls

⑫

Canyon

Teewinot
Mountain

Glacier

Saddle

Delta
Lake

Amphitheater
Lake
9698

Surprise
Lake

AMPHITHEATER

Pinnacle

Cleft
Falls

Mount
Owen
12928

East
Prong

Teton
Glacier

Disappointment
Peak

Garnet

Meadow

Spalding
Falls

Teepe Gl

Glacier

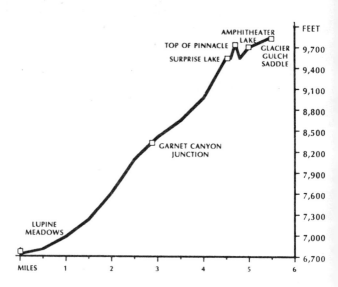

The trail begins in a southerly direction following the base of the mountains. For the first .3 miles, you get intermittent views of the sagebrush biotic community on the left. A "biotic community" may be defined as distinct, organized groupings of living organisms (both plant and animal) inhabiting areas with differing physical characteristics, such as elevation, soil composition, water availability and sun exposure. The coarse-textured soil left behind by glacial outwash activity is principally responsible for the existence of the sagebrush community here and throughout the valley floor. Because the soil contains very little loam, it does not retain moisture well. To survive, plants must be able to adapt to the arid environment. The dominant plant is low sagebrush, a fragrant grayish-green shrub with small yellow flowers, which bloom in late August. It provides important forage for antelope, elk, mule deer, moose, Uinta ground squirrels and sage grouse.

Another factor partially responsible for the existence of Jackson Hole's extensive sagebrush community is a "rain shadow" cast by the Teton Range. As the prevailing southwest winds approach the Tetons from the Idaho side, air is forced upward. The water vapor contained in the rising air cools and condenses into clouds and often falls as rain or snow on the western side of the mountains. Having "milked" the clouds of their moisture, the Tetons cast a "shadow" of dry air over Jackson Hole.

As the valley gives way to the forest, the complex population of living organisms changes. Here along the well-drained lower mountain scopes exists a biotic community dominated by the lodgepole pine which can be identified by its tall, straight slender trunk. These trees were commonly used by Indians in constructing their tepees or lodges, hence the name "lodgepole." They sometimes grow so close together they block the sunlight needed to support smaller plants and animals which otherwise would inhabit the forest floor, creating what's known as a "lodgepole desert." The trees in this area are spaced farther apart and support a rich population of rodents, including red squirrel, pocket gopher and deer mouse, as well as their nemesis, the crafty pine marten. Also present are birds such as the Clark's nutcracker, ruffed grouse and the great gray owl. Larger animals include moose, elk, mule deer, coyote and black bear.

Soon the trail crosses a rushing creek fed by meltwater from Teton Glacier which lies 4,000 feet above you at the head of Glacier Gulch. Often the water is milky white due to a fine-grained sediment resulting from the abrasion of rock by the glacier. This sediment is called "glacial flour." Glaciers form when more snow falls each winter than is melted each summer. Over many years, the snow accumulates and compacts into ice. As this glacial ice grows, gravity causes it to move down-valley like a mighty river of ice. It is this movement across the mountain's surface which is responsible for the carving, scratching, and sculpturing action distinguishing a true glacier from a stationary ice field. Teton Glacier, the largest of 12 active glaciers in the park, has an advance rate of approximately 30 feet per year. Considering the glacier is almost a mile long, it is possible that the meltwater flowing beneath you fell as snow near the top of Teton Glacier over 100 years ago.

After 1.7 miles and a 700 foot raise in elevation, a trail junction is reached. As you continue ahead toward Amphitheater Lake, the trail enters a series of 18 switchbacks and climbs more than 2,000 feet in the next 2.7 miles. Along the way, the trail passes through three biotic communities. The first few right-turn-switchbacks tend to occur on south-facing slopes which are exposed to the full force of the summer sun and desiccating southwesterly winds. These physical conditions support a sporadic Douglas fir community, particularly at the lower elevations. Look for a Douglas fir tree just to the left of the trail at the third switchback. Its most distinctive feature is its female cone, which contains three-pronged, feather-like bracts between the scales. Animals which call the Douglas fir community home include a number of rodents and a rich diversity of birds such as woodpeckers, sapsuckers, chickadees, nuthatches, and the great horned owl.

The left-turn-switchbacks mostly occur in cooler, moister north-facing slopes which support a spruce-fir community. The dominant trees here are Engelmann spruce and subalpine fir. The fir trees can be distinguished from the spruce by their flat, flexible needles and erect cones. The spruce have sharp needles and short downward hanging cones. In between the switchbacks are open east-facing slopes that support a sagebrush community similar to one in the valley below. It is interesting to note that these three separate communities all exist at the same elevation. Although elevation is an important factor, other physical characteristics are clearly more important here.

At the 3 mile mark (8,400' elevation), a spur trail to Garnet Canyon is passed (see hike #12 in this guide for a description). At 4.4 miles, the trail levels out and affords brief views of the Grand Teton (13,770') and surrounding mountains. Another .2 miles takes you to beautiful Surprise Lake (9,540'). As you probably have noticed, the vegetation has again changed. You have now entered the lower reaches of the alpine tundra community. This community extends in elevation up to the top of the highest peaks in the park. Around Surprise Lake the dominant vegetation is the five-needled whitebark pine, mixed with a few spruce and fir trees. At higher elevations, the community is dominated by dwarf whitebark pine trees, shrubs, a variety of delicate wildflowers and many colorful crustose lichens which cling to rock surfaces.

For the best views of Surprise Lake, follow the foot trail along the east shore to the outlet on the far side. And for one of the most spectacular views of the Tetons anywhere, you should scramble another 200 feet in elevation up "Surprise Lake Pinnacle" which lies just southeast of the lake. The best route up the pinnacle begins at the lakeshore near the outlet.

The top of Surprise Lake Pinnacle affords a dramatic panorama of naked Teton peaks which cut like shark's teeth against the sky. Where most see a string of rugged peaks, some see a race track. In 1963, virtually every peak in this area was topped in just over 20 hours, in what has come to be known as the "Teton Summits Endurance Run." Three men began at their car shortly before midnight. Then, in order from left to right, they scaled wicked- looking Nez Perce Peak (3:15 a.m.), continued west across Cloudveil Dome (5 a.m.) and South Teton (6:30 a.m.), then north over Middle Teton, with its distinctive black dike (9 a.m.), the Grand (10:30 a.m.) and Mount Owen (1:45 p.m.), and finally east over Teewinot (6 p.m.) before returning to their car at 8 p.m.

Another .2 miles past Surprise Lake is beautiful Amphitheater Lake (9,698'). Both lakes lie in bowl-shaped cirques, steep-walled amphitheaters formed as a result of erosion which occurred near the head of a mighty glacier. Before returning down the mountain, take time to relax and to do a little exploring; you've earned it! The trail continues along the eastern shore of Amphitheater Lake, then climbs another 150 feet in elevation to a saddle overlooking Glacier Gulch. The views of the massive gray-colored moraine which lies below Teton Glacier and the dramatic views down U-shaped Glacier Gulch make this worth the extra effort. There are no official trails beyond this point. Persons interested in mountain climbing should inquire at one of the local mountaineering schools.

> *For* the Grand Teton National Park is preeminently the national park of mountain peaks—*the Park of Matterhorns.*
>
> —Fritiof M. Fryxell, the Park's First Ranger-Naturalist

⑫ GARNET CANYON

Hiking up Garnet Canyon toward Middle Teton.

TRAILHEAD: The trail begins at Lupine Meadows. To reach the trailhead, drive 7.5 miles north of Moose Junction, or 1 mile south of South Jenny Lake Junction, on the Teton Park Road, turn west on the unpaved spur-road marked "Lupine Meadows Trailhead," and continue 1.6 miles to a parking area. (GPS: 43° 44' 05" N, 110° 44' 27" W)

DISTANCE: 10 miles (round-trip).

ELEVATION CHANGES: 2,650 feet.

TIME REQUIRED: 6 hours.

DIFFICULTY: Strenuous.

COMMENTS: This hike takes you up Garnet Canyon, through a boulder field to a beautiful high mountain meadow nestled among the lofty Teton summits. Snow can be a problem until midsummer. The official trail ends at the boulder field. **For a map of this hike turn to the Amphitheater Lake hike (#11 in this guide book).**

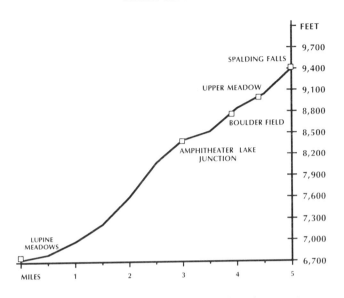

From Lupine Meadows the trail travels south and soon begins to rise. At the 1.7 mile mark you have climbed 700 feet. Here the Valley Trail splits off to the left, while the trail to Garnet Canyon continues to climb along a morainal ridge then enters a series of steep switchbacks. A short distance past the fifth switchback, the trail divides. Garnet Canyon lies to the left. At this junction you have traveled 3 miles and gained over 1,600 feet in elevation. For a more detailed description of many of the interesting sights seen along this first 3 mile stretch of trail turn to the Amphitheater Lake hike (#11 in this guide book).

From the trail junction, the Garnet Canyon trail breaks quickly out of the trees and heads straight for imposing Nez Perce Peak (11,901'), named in honor of the proud Indian tribe which traveled this part of the Rocky Mountains. The Nez Perce (French for "pierced nose") are most often remembered for their skillful and valiant 1877 fighting retreat from the U.S. Cavalry. Driven to warfare by the pressure of land greed, they made a 1,300 mile flight across the west in a failed attempt to reach Canada and safety.

Far below you on the left are Bradley and Taggart lakes, named for Frank Bradley and W.R. Taggart, two geologist members of the 1872 Hayden Geological Survey. On closer scrutiny, you can spot the effects of the Beaver Creek forest fire which reached Taggart Lake, but fell short of Bradley Lake. In August of 1985, a lightning-caused forest fire ripped through this area, burning over 1,000 acres before it was contained.

As the trail bends to the right and starts up Garnet Canyon, Middle Teton (12,804') comes into view. It lies at the head of the canyon and can be easily distinguished by the conspicuous black ribbon-like column cutting vertically through the mountain. This distinctive geological feature is a "dike," formed when molten magma welled up into a fissure in the older Precambrian rock. When the magma cooled, it formed a dark-colored, low-silica rock known as "diabase." The diabase dike exposed on the face of Middle Teton is 20-to-40 feet wide and runs east-west through the mountain for more than a mile.

Garnet Canyon takes its name from another interesting geologic feature. If you are lucky, you may spot a reddish-brown garnet crystal imbedded in white pegmatite rock. Most crystals range in size from a BB shot to a small marble; however, some are larger than a baseball. Although Teton garnets have no gemstone value, they have great educational and historical worth. Remember, collecting specimens is strictly forbidden.

At the 4.1 mile mark the Garnet Canyon trail officially ends as it enters a boulder field. However, a climber's path continues another .5 miles to a beautiful alpine meadow surrounded by the spectacular Teton summits. Its not too tough to scramble through the boulder field once the snow melts in July. The climber's trail which traverses the boulder field parallels closely Garnet Creek. Along the banks of the creek, you may see delicate pink Lewis monkeyflowers or the intricate red willowherb. The meadow is dominated by sedges, grasses and low shrubs, with a splash of pink provided by the fluffy-flowered subalpine spirea. Try not to step on anything green. This beautiful, but delicate meadow is struggling hard against the elements to survive.

At the head of the meadow is beautiful Spalding Falls, named for Bishop Frank Spalding who in 1898 accompanied William Owen on what was most likely the first successful ascent of the Grand Teton (13,770'). To this day, however, a controversy continues as to who was the first to climb the Grand. Nathaniel P. Langford claimed that he and another member of the Hayden Survey, James Stevenson, climbed the Grand in 1872. Owen, convinced that he had been the first, spent over 30 years lobbying for his climbing party to be declared the first to have conquered the Grand. Then in 1929, possibly through some backroom politicking, the Wyoming Legislature by joint resolution declared Owen the winner. Today, dozens of later-day-explorers make the ascent each day. Many use this meadow as a base camp. Travel beyond the meadow is restricted to those with proper training and equipment. If you are interested in mountain climbing, you should inquire at one of the local mountaineering schools.

The early inexcessability of many Teton peaks made it difficult to map this area. Cartographers in the late 1800's located points through the use of triangulation, the geometric principle that a triangle consists of six parts (3 angles and 3 sides), and if you can discover any three parts then you can calculate the other three. Elevations were calculated through the use of mercurial barometers calibrated at points of known elevation. Unfortunately, the best place from which to take measurements is the top of the highest peaks. Since most of the Teton peaks were not scaled until the 1920's, early mapping necessarily involved considerable guess work, as well as the use of crude instruments. Maps published as late as the 1930's contained elevation errors exceeding 500 feet. Today, laser beams and satellites can locate points within a centimeter and elevations can be determined within a foot.

> *Climb the mountains and get their good tidings. Nature's peace will flow into you as sunshine flows into trees. The winds will blow their own freshness into you, and the storms their energy, while cares will drop off like autumn leaves.*
>
> —John Muir

⑬ LAKE SOLITUDE

Gazing down North Cascade Canyon toward the "Cathedral Group."

TRAILHEAD: The easiest way to reach the trailhead is via an inexpensive shuttle boat which departs from Jenny Lake's East Shore Boat Dock approximately every 20 minutes from 8 a.m. to 6 p.m. during summer months. The East Shore Boat Dock is located near Jenny Lake Ranger Station, 8 miles north of Moose Junction on the west side of the Teton Park Road. You can skip the boat and walk around Jenny Lake. However, that adds 2 miles to the hike, each way. (GPS @ East Shore Boat Dock: 43° 45' 05" N, 110° 43' 20" W)

DISTANCE: 14.8 miles (round-trip).

ELEVATION CHANGES: 2,300 feet.

TIME REQUIRED: 8 hours (plus boat rides).

DIFFICULTY: Strenuous.

COMMENTS: This hike does not afford much "solitude," but it will expose you to some of the most spectacular alpine scenery anywhere. Snow is a problem early in the summer. Later in the season, the wildflowers are wonderful. For additional information, purchase an inexpensive flier titled "Cascade Canyon Trail," at NPS Visitor Centers.

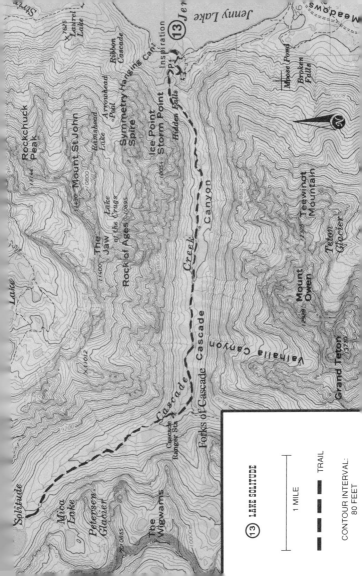

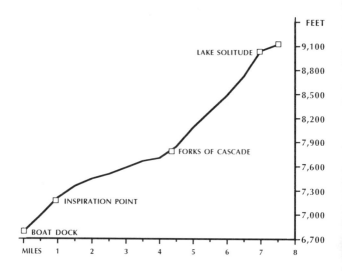

After disembarking the shuttle boat at the West Shore Boat Dock, the trail turns left and gradually climbs .5 miles to Hidden Falls, then switchbacks another .5 miles to impressive Inspiration Point. For a detailed description of many of the interesting sights seen along this first stretch of trail turn to the Hidden Falls/Inspiration Point hike (#5 in this guide book).

As you continue past Inspiration Point, you get an impressive view of the "Cathedral Group" of peaks—from left to right, Teewinot Mountain (12,325'), Grand Teton (13,770') and Mount Owen (12,928'). It is not unusual to find natural features in America compared to old world architecture such as castles or cathedrals. Early in our history, Americans agonized over our relative lack of historical literature, architecture and art. To compensate, as a nation we turned to the spectacular natural wonders of the North American West for a scenic heritage in which to take pride.

As you continue up Cascade Canyon the lofty Teton summits tower more than a mile above you on the left. Along the way you traverse the base of several large open rock outcroppings which seem to cascade down from your right. These outcroppings are made up of millions of broken rocks (or talus), which were pried from the canyon walls above you through a slow but constant erosive process. The process begins with stress and strain on the rock caused by the minute contraction and expansion resulting from temperature fluxuations. Cracks form in the rock, water seeps in, and through repeated freezing and thawing eventually a slab breaks away from the mountain.

The talus slopes provide excellent homes for the tiny pika (or rock rabbit). Listen for its forceful "bleats" and watch for piles of grass which it collects and spreads to dry. Once dried, the grass will be stored for winter in a den beneath the rocks. Watch, also, for the larger and less reclusive yellowbellied marmot, often seen sunning on the rocks. The marmot, which also lives in underground dens, is one of the park's only hibernators. During the winter, they "power down" their metabolism. Their body temperature drops to almost freezing, their heart beats only 4 times each minute and they enter a deep coma-like sleep. Thus the pika and the marmot, in their own unique way, have found a means of surviving winter in the Tetons.

In August, this hike is a berry pickers' paradise. The open rock areas are teaming with wild raspberry plants. Its berries are smaller, but more flavorful then cultivated raspberries. In the forest, look for wild huckleberries, a two to three-foot high bushy shrub which bears a plethora of delicious reddish-purple berries, and for grouse whortle-berries, a six to eight-inch high light green shrub with tiny egg-shaped leaves and minute but flavorful red berries. It is legal to eat wild berries in national parks. However, you should never eat berries unless you are confident of their identity.

At the 4.5 mile mark the trail forks. To the right, the north fork trail continues to climb more than 1,200 feet in the next 2.5 miles to the shores of Lake Solitude (9,035'). About a half-mile beyond the trail junction, you begin to break out of the spruce-fir forest and the rare beauty of North Cascade Canyon unfolds before you. Ahead, the meadows on the floor of the broad glacier-carved canyon rise grace-fully to meet the canyon walls. Behind you, the Grand Teton looks ominous and appears to grow higher and higher as you continue your climb. The wildflowers are spectacular. In early July, fields of delicate yellow glacier lilies abound almost as soon as the snow melts. Later in the summer, moist areas surrounding the many small streams in the canyon support the prominent pink Lewis monkeyflower; the aptly-named monkshood, with its distinctive purple flowers forming a hood-shaped structure; the delicate mountain bluebell, with its clusters of tiny blue flowers hanging down from long stems; and the intricate cream-colored columbine, with its five conspicuous hollow spurs extending behind the flower.

Lake Solitude is reached at the 7 mile mark. However, for the best views, you should pass by the crowds and continue to the far side of the lake before resting. The lake covers approximately 50 acres and measures 25 feet at its deepest point. It is one of the largest lakes in the park for its elevation and is arguably the most beautiful.

Lake Solitude, like Jenny Lake far below in Jackson Hole, owes its existence to glacial action. However, they were created in very different ways. The moraine surrounding Jenny Lake marks the glacier's furthest point of growth before it receded. Lake Solitude, on the other hand, lies in a glacial depression at the base of a geologic "cirque," a semicircular hollow or amphitheater eroded in the mountain where the glacier began. Thus, Lake Solitude, in a sense, marks the birthplace of the glacier and Jenny Lake marks the end of its adventuresome travels. The rock which was eroded away from the mountain to form this beautiful cirque was transported down Cascade Canyon by the glacier. Today, that same rock may make up part of the moraine which helped create Jenny Lake.

Take time and enjoy yourself at Lake Solitude. But, remember the last boat departs the West Shore Boat Dock at 6:00 p.m. Therefore, unless you are willing to hike the extra two miles, you should plan your time accordingly. Also, leave yourself enough time to enjoy the return trip. Although it is the same trail, in many respects it is a different hike.

⑭ TABLE MOUNTAIN

Lofty Teton summits rise above square-topped Table Mountain.

TRAILHEAD: The trail begins at Teton Campground in Grand Targhee National Forest on the Idaho side of the Tetons. To reach the trailhead from Jackson, Wyoming: take Highway 22 west over Teton Pass to Victor, Idaho; turn north on Highway 33 and travel 8 miles to Driggs, Idaho; at the main intersection in Driggs, turn right onto "Little Ave" (look for a sign pointing to Grand Targhee Ski Resort) and proceed 6 miles; make another right onto the unpaved road marked "Teton Campground" and continue five more miles to the end. Look for the trailhead sign marked "North Teton Trail" at the far side of the campground. (GPS: 43° 45' 25" N, 110° 55' 03" W)

DISTANCE: 12 miles (round-trip).

ELEVATION CHANGES: Table Mountain stands 4,100 feet above the trailhead. Good Luck!

TIME REQUIRED: 8 hours.

DIFFICULTY: Very strenuous.

COMMENTS: This strenuous hike ascends over 4,000 feet to the top of Table Mountain (11,106') and affords what many believe is the best view of the Teton Range. Snow can be a problem until midsummer. Also, it's a good idea to take a jacket or wind-breaker on this trip.

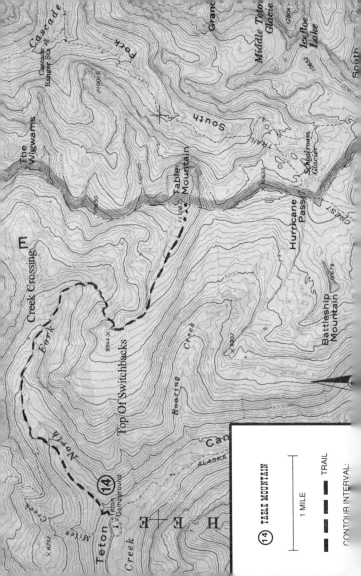

Grand
Middle Teton Glacier
IceFloe Lake
South
Cascade
Fork
Cascade Ranger Sta
10075
South
TRAIL
Schoolroom Glacier
The Wigwams
Table Mountain
9650
10635
11106
Hurricane Pass
CREST
Battleship Mountain
10679
Creek Crossing
Fork
9200
9200
9944 ×
Top Of Switchbacks
× 9407
Roaring
Creek
Teton
North
8000
Cascade
Can
Campground
ALASKA
Creek
× 8252
Teton Creek

(14) TABLE MOUNTAIN

1 MILE

——— TRAIL

CONTOUR INTERVAL:

TABLE MOUNTAIN

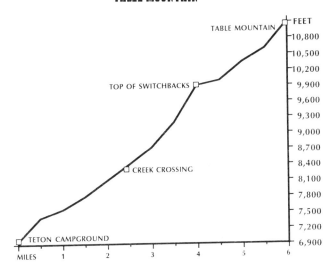

Except for the top of Table Mountain, which lies on the western edge of Grand Teton National Park, this entire hike is in Grand Targhee National Forest, named in honor of Chief Targhee of the Shoshone Indian Nation. Unlike national park land, which is preserved for "The Benefit and Enjoyment of the People," national forest land is set aside for its "many uses," which may include logging, mining, oil exploration and other commercial enterprise. Fortunately, much of the more beautiful and ecologically significant forest land, including the area you are entering, has now been designated "Wilderness Area" and is not subject to such uses.

From the campground, the trail quickly climbs 400 feet in the first half mile, then levels a bit as it parallels the north fork of Teton Creek. Soon, you cross into the Jedediah Smith Wilderness Area, created as part of Grand Targhee National Forest in 1984. Jedediah, one of the most interesting figures of the Rocky Mountain fur trade era, answered an 1822 St. Louis newspaper advertisement calling for "enterprising young men . . . to ascend the River Missouri to its source, there to be employed for one, two or three years." He quickly grew in stature. As a mountain man he was unsurpassed, successfully leading trapping parties through perilous territory. As an explorer he excelled, forging the first passage over the Sierra Nevada Mountains to the Pacific Ocean. A deeply religious man, he did not swear, drink, or use tobacco and he always carried his Bible. Jedediah lost part of an ear to a grizzly and eventually his life to a Comanche spear, but he never lost the respect of his men or his faith in God.

Just past the 1 mile mark, look for moose in the open meadows and among the tall, shrubby willows which thrive near the creek to the right. The tender leaves and twigs of the willows make up a large portion of the moose's diet. In fact, the name "moose" comes from the Algonquin Indian term meaning twig eater. At the 2.5 mile mark the trail crosses the creek on a small footbridge. Black bear are often seen in this area. Bear cubs are born in January when the female is still asleep in her den. A newborn cub may weigh as little as just 8 ounces, which is remarkable when compared to its mother's weight of 150 to 250 pounds. Healthy females usually give birth to one or two cubs every other year. Just ahead on the left, you will find a large granite outcropping which is a nice spot to rest. At this point you have climbed 1,000 feet. To the southeast, you can now see gently sloping Table Mountain rising another 3,000 feet to its distinctive box-shaped top.

As you near the 3.5 mile mark, the trail bends to the right and enters a series of 9 switchbacks which climb 1,000 feet in less than a mile. Early in the season snow can be a problem in this area. Later in the summer, hikers on the lower switchbacks are treated to a beautiful display of wildflowers including: the prominent pink Lewis monkeyflower; the well-named monkshood, with its distinctive purple flowers forming a hood-shaped structure; the fiery red-topped Indian paintbrush; and the delicate mountain bluebell, with it's clusters of tiny blue flowers hanging down from long stems. As you climb the switchbacks, you begin to see the mighty summits of the Teton Range as they, peak over the ridge to the east. First you see the Grand (13,770') then to its right, the Middle Teton (12,804') and to its left, Mount Owen (12,928'). Finally, far to the right you see the South Teton (12,514'). From this western vantage, the so-called "back side" of the Tetons, one can understand how the lonely French fur trappers, upon seeing these majestic peaks silhouetted against the sky, allowed their minds to wander and fondly dubbed them "Les Trois Tetons" (the three breasts).

The elevation at the top of the ridge above the switchbacks is 9,944 feet. Here, the summer growing season is short and the winter conditions are severe. The only trees that can survive are the gnarled whitebark pines and even they cannot grow much further up the mountain. The climate is cool, moist and often windy. The soil is scant and supports a sparse population of shrubs and flowers. This is the biotic community known as alpine tundra. From here, the top of Table Mountain looks deceptively close. Actually, its almost two miles away and another 1,000 feet up. As you continue up the broad, sloping meadow, try not to step on anything green. These plants struggle enough against the elements without also doing battle with your feet.

The box-shaped top of Table Mountain, which gives the mountain its name, is made up of sedimentary rock. Millions of years ago, many layers of sedimentary rock formed an unbroken horizontal blanket covering the older Precambrian basement rocks beneath. Approximately 9 million years ago, the Teton Range faulted up, exposing these hard basement rocks, which today make up the core of the Tetons. Subsequent erosion stripped away much of the sedimentary rock, leaving relatively few areas, like Table Mountain, exposed. Be very careful as you make the final ascent through this sedimentary rock. It is really just a consolidated accumulation of sand, rock and shell fragments and therefore, is brittle, crumbly and difficult to climb.

From the top of Table Mountain you feel as though you are standing shoulder to shoulder with the clouds. No words can describe this breathtaking view. Suffice it to say that in 1872, famous photographer William H. Jackson, searching for the perfect spot from which to make the first photographs ever of the Tetons, chose Table Mountain as his vantage. If you think it was tough getting up here, imagine how difficult it was for Jackson, who traveled for nine days without benefit of a blazed trail, leading his mule, "Molly," packed high with bulky cameras, lenses, tripods, glass plates, chemicals and a makeshift darkroom. But it was all worth it. Even with the crude photographic equipment of the day, the images which Jackson captured from the top of Table Mountain remain unsurpassed!

Before descending the mountain, closely survey the landscape for bighorn sheep. This is one of the few hikes in the Tetons where you have a fair chance to view these beautiful animals. Although related to domestic sheep, the bighorn has a coat of hair, not wool. Both the male (ram) and the female (ewe) have horns which are never shed.

⑮ MARION LAKE/GRANITE CANYON

Flower-filled alpine meadows line the trail to Marion Lake.

TRAILHEAD: This trail begins at the top of the aerial tram at the Jackson Hole Ski Area, 21 miles from the town of Jackson, Wyoming. From Jackson, take Highway 22 west (toward Teton Pass), turn right on the Teton Village Road and follow the signs to the ski area. A large double reversible tram will take you to the top of Rendezvous Mountain (10,450'). There is a charge for the tram which typically operates 8 a.m. to 7 p.m. during peak summer season. (GPS @ base of tram: 43° 35' 17" N, 110° 49' 39" W)

DISTANCE: 15.5 miles (round-trip).

ELEVATION CHANGES: Overall there is a drop of 4,100 feet from the top of the tram to Teton Village. There is some up and down on this trail, causing you to climb a cumulative 1,300 feet. But it is never more than 400 feet at a time.

TIME REQUIRED: 8 hours (plus a tram ride).

DIFFICULTY: Strenuous.

COMMENTS: This hike begins at the top of the aerial tram and ends at the base of the tram. It gives hikers an opportunity to enjoy spectacular alpine scenery without the usual climb. But do not be fooled, this is still a tough hike. At this elevation, snow conditions can be a real problem until midsummer.

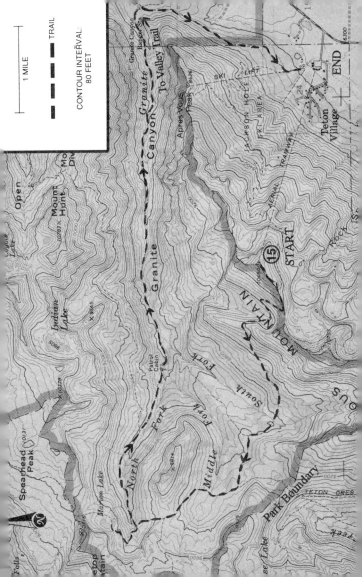

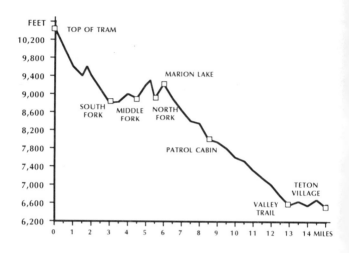

From the top of the tram, turn left and follow a well-beaten trail southwest, toward "Cody Bowl" and "Granite Canyon Trailhead." A detailed description of many of the more interesting sights along this first section of trail is contained in the Rendezvous Mountain hike (#4 in this guide book).

At the .5 mile mark, you reach the turnoff for the Granite Canyon and Marion Lake trail. Turn right and follow this trail as it enters Grand Teton National Park and then drops quickly off the mountain ridge. Notice how the vegetation has changed. This northwest facing slope receives less direct sunlight and wind than the top of the ridge. Engelmann spruce and the subalpine fir are the dominant trees in this cool, moist environment. Such conditions also prevent the winter snows from melting in this area until well into July, which can cause problems for hikers.

As you break out of the trees, the late summer display of wildflowers is spectacular. The moist areas surrounding the many small streams in this area support mountain bluebell (with its clusters of tiny blue flowers hanging down from long stems), fringed gentian (with its beautiful two-inch long tubular shaped purple flowers trumpeting skyward), and elephanthead (growing in two-foot stocks covered with delicate pinkish-purple flowers, each of which remarkably resembles the head, ears and trunk of an elephant). The trail climbs up and over a small ridge and crosses the South Fork of Granite Creek before reaching a trail junction at the 3.5 mile mark. Turn left and continue following signs to Marion Lake. At the 4.1 mile mark the trail merges with the Teton Crest Trail. Bear right and follow the Crest Trail as it drops to a crossing of the Middle Fork, then begins a 300 foot climb through a beautiful alpine meadow.

The gray cliffs that loom above you on the left are the protruding edges of many layers of sedimentary rock that accumulated in shallow seas periodically existing here during the geologic period known as the Paleozoic Era (600 million to 250 million years ago). The most distinctive part of this ridge is jagged-edged Housetop Mountain (10,537') that lies ahead of you on the left. Also of interest are the numerous boulders, some over 10 feet high, lying scattered about the meadow. Notice the sedimentary layers in these rocks. They obviously broke away from the cliffs above. Sedimentary rock, like that exposed in this area, occasionally contains fossils of tiny marine organisms such as brachiopods which inhabited the seas millions of years before life developed on land.

From the top of the meadow the views down Granite Canyon are excellent. In August, the fields of lupine, a distant relative of the Texas bluebonnet, are incredible. Years ago lupine lotion made from these flowers was successfully used to combat body lice. They also have a delightful fragrance which permeates the meadow. In addition, you may notice small narrow dirt piles running along the ground in this area. This is the handiwork of the pocket gopher. In the winter these small animals burrow underground and pack the excess dirt into tunnels they dig in the snow. When the snow melts, these mounds of dirt are exposed. From here, the trail drops 400 feet down another heavily timbered north slope, crosses the North Fork of Granite Creek and then switchbacks 300 feet up the other side.

At the 5.9 mile mark you reach beautiful emerald-colored Marion Lake (9,240'), named for Ms. Marion Danford, early owner of the D Triangle Ranch in Jackson Hole. This is a great spot to rest a spell and enjoy the scenery and the symphony of life which surrounds the lake. Listen for the distinctive, shrill "chirp" of the yellowbellied marmot. These 5 to 10 pound rodents easily attain a length of two feet, counting their short bushy tail. They live in underground dens beneath the rocks and are some of the park's only hibernators. During the winter they "power down" their metabolism. Their body temperature drops to almost freezing, their heart beats only 4 times each minute and they enter a deep coma-like sleep. In this way, they conserve energy and can survive until spring.

Listen also for the chattering of the red squirrel. These vociferous creatures relish the seed-bearing cones from the spruce, fir and whitebark pine trees in the area. Look around the base of the trees for piles of cone scales left behind where the squirrels have been feeding. The squirrel survives through its quickness and intelligence. They are known to scout their territory, testing every possible escape route. Although they appear playful, they must be constantly vigilant to elude the crafty pine marten which also lives here. This long, sleek, short-legged animal with a tiny fox-like face and brown bushy tail is a formidable predator, feeding principally on small rodents. The loud "kerr, kerr" sounds of the Clark's nutcracker are also common around Marion Lake. They too enjoy whitebark pine nuts, but would just as soon steal a meal from your pack.

Before leaving the Marion Lake area, walk out to the campsite located on the bluff southeast of the lake. There you get a magnificent view down Granite Canyon, your return route to Teton Village. It's tough to leave such a beautiful spot, but the nearly 10 miles which lie ahead of you requires that you keep moving. First, drop back down to the trail junction you passed near the crossing of the North Fork. Turn left and follow the trail as it gradually descends Granite Canyon through open meadows and intermittent areas of willows and forest. At the 7.7 mile mark, you pass the Open Canyon Trail junction, then at 8.4 miles you pass the junction with the Middle Fork Cutoff Trail.

As you continue to descend the canyon, the Engelmann spruce and subalpine fir trees make room for Douglas fir, lodgepole pine and even a stand or two of cottonwood trees near the bottom. Along the way the trail passes through a number of rock slides. Notice how the light and dark-colored portions of some rocks separate into bands. This hard rock formation is known as Layered Gneiss (pronounced "nice"), a metamorphic rock that formed under extreme heat and pressure. Under such conditions, the rock became taffy-like and was bent and folded into unusual designs which can be seen along the trail. Apparently "Granite" Canyon was mistakenly named for this rock. Although both rocks are composed of the same basic minerals, granite is an igneous rock and does not usually appear banded.

Look for wild raspberry plants among the rocks. This member of the rose family bears fruit in July and August. Its tiny berries are even more flavorful than larger cultivated berries. The National Park Service does allow the picking of berries, but the birds may beat you to the good ones!

At the 13.1 mile mark, you reach the Valley Trail. Teton Village lies another 2.4 miles to the right. The trail travels up and over several small hills and enters the base of the ski area via a service road.

Oh Lord, how manifold are thy works! In wisdom hast thou made them all; the earth is full of thy riches.

—Psalms 104:24